# C# Programming for Absolute Beginners

Radek Vystavěl

Apress®

## *C# Programming for Absolute Beginners*

Radek Vystavěl
Ondřejov, Czech Republic

ISBN-13 (pbk): 978-1-4842-3317-7           ISBN-13 (electronic): 978-1-4842-3318-4
https://doi.org/10.1007/978-1-4842-3318-4

Library of Congress Control Number: 2017962139

Cover image designed by Freepik

Managing Director: Welmoed Spahr
Editorial Director: Todd Green
Acquisitions Editor: Gwenan Spearing
Development Editor: Laura Berendson
Technical Reviewer: Fabio Ferracchiati and Sean Whitesell
Coordinating Editor: Nancy Chen
Copy Editor: KimWimpsett
Compositor: SPi Global
Indexer: SPi Global
Artist: SPi Global

Distributed to the book trade worldwide by Springer Science+Business Media New York, 233 Spring Street, 6th Floor, New York, NY 10013. Phone 1-800-SPRINGER, fax (201) 348-4505, e-mail orders-ny@springer-sbm.com, or visit www.springeronline.com. Apress Media, LLC is a California LLC and the sole member (owner) is Springer Science + Business Media Finance Inc (SSBM Finance Inc). SSBM Finance Inc is a **Delaware** corporation.

For information on translations, please e-mail rights@apress.com, or visit www.apress.com/rights-permissions.

Apress titles may be purchased in bulk for academic, corporate, or promotional use. eBook versions and licenses are also available for most titles. For more information, reference our Print and eBook Bulk Sales web page at www.apress.com/bulk-sales.

Any source code or other supplementary material referenced by the author in this book is available to readers on GitHub via the book's product page, located at www.apress.com/9781484233177. For more detailed information, please visit www.apress.com/source-code.

Printed on acid-free paper

*To my parents whose loving care allowed me to live an untroubled childhood and to develop my talents in exact sciences. Let this book be a celebration of their efforts, not having been, hopefully, in vain.*

*Mým rodičům, jejichž láskyplná péče mi umožnila prožít bezstarostné dětství a rozvinout nadání pro exaktní vědy. Ať je tato kniha oslavou jejich úsilí, které, doufám, nepřišlo vniveč.*

# Table of Contents

# About the Author

**Radek Vystavěl** is a software developer based in Ondřejov, Czech Republic. During his career, he has helped many companies and academic institutions with their demands for tailor-made software. In addition, in the past 15 years, he has taught many courses about programming and databases, both at the college level and through his own events. During this time, he has acquired substantial experience teaching beginners and has decided to share it with a worldwide audience. In his leisure time, he studies physics and its history and draws his inspiration from walking in the woods and meadows.

# About the Technical Reviewers

**Fabio Claudio Ferracchiati** is a senior consultant and a senior analyst/developer using Microsoft technologies. He works at BluArancio S.p.A (`www.bluarancio.com`) as a senior analyst/developer and Microsoft Dynamics CRM specialist. He is a Microsoft Certified Solution Developer for .NET, a Microsoft Certified Application Developer for .NET, a Microsoft Certified Professional, and a prolific author and technical reviewer. Over the past ten years, he's written articles for Italian and international magazines and has co-authored more than ten books on a variety of computer topics.

**Sean Whitesell** is a software developer in Tulsa, Oklahoma, with more than 17 years of experience in client-server, web, embedded, and electronics development. He is the president of the Tulsa .NET User Group and frequently speaks at area user groups and conferences. His passions are solving problems programmatically, coding craftsmanship, and teaching. He is also a chaplain and sound engineer at his church and teaches self-defense classes to children.

# Acknowledgments

Special thanks to my daughter, Amálie, who assisted me in preparing the manuscript. She typed a large portion of it and prepared many figures, upon my instruction.

Thanks also to the whole Apress team, technical reviewers included, whose expertise and drive allowed the book to be completed properly and on time. Especially I appreciate the e-mail discussions with Gwenan Spearing concerning the philosophy of the book, as well as her suggestions, which substantially improved it. Also, the book got much better due to the hard work of Kim Wimpsett, who kindly polished my English.

# CHAPTER 1

# Getting Ready

Welcome, dear reader, as you begin your journey to learn programming! Computers, tablets, mobile phones, and many other electronic devices are programmable and will do exactly what a human programmer tells them to do.

Programming is a world based entirely on logic. In this respect, it is quite unique among human activities. If you like logic—for example, you like solving puzzles or you are accustomed to searching for the meaningful order around you—then you will love programming.

## C# Language

In this book, you will create some real programs, and for this purpose, you need to learn a programming language, which is what gives the computer its instructions. Programming languages provide the interaction between computers and humans. They are strict enough so that absolutely dumb computers can understand them, and yet they are human enough so that programmers can write code using them.

Over time, many programming languages have been created, and many are in use today. Each language has its virtues and drawbacks.

For this book, I have chosen the C# programming language, which is my number-one language both for professional development and for teaching. It's about 15 years old, which means its creators could avoid the known flaws of older languages when developing it. In addition, it is now a time-proven language, not to be readily replaced by some new fashion.

C# is actually the flagship language of Microsoft. It is quite universal—you can use it to write a variety of programs ranging from traditional console and desktop applications through web sites and services to mobile development, both for business and for entertainment. Originally born on Windows, it has been quickly spreading onto other platforms in recent years—such as Linux and Mac and Android and iOS.

1

© Radek Vystavěl 2017
R. Vystavěl, *C# Programming for Absolute Beginners*, https://doi.org/10.1007/978-1-4842-3318-4_1

I hope you will have a good time with it and you will find many uses for it in your future professional/hobby life!

# Who This Book For

The book is primarily intended for those who have no or only a limited knowledge of programming. To get the most from this book, you should be skillful with computers—you should be able to install a program, know what a file or a folder is, and so on.

However, because of the book's deep coverage of the topics included, you may also benefit from the book if you are an intermediate programmer or someone who has already mastered another programming language and want to start with C#. You will simply proceed faster through the book than absolute beginners.

# How the Book Differs from Others

I wrote this book based on my 15 years of experience teaching programming to various groups of students, teachers, hobbyists, and others. For many of them, it was their first encounter with the subject. I watched them closely while working, and over the years I have accumulated a fair amount of information about how people learn, what is easy for them, and what requires more attention.

In this book, you will benefit from this knowledge. The book differs from similar ones mostly in the following aspects:

- The pace of explanations—i.e., the speed of proceeding to new topics—is appropriately slow so that you do not get lost shortly after having started. A common fallacy of expert authors is to consider beginner stuff as trivial. Actually, it *is* trivial—for them. But not for the reader. I have made considerable effort to avoid this and to spend enough time on things considered easy by the initiated.

- I believe that for you to successfully grasp all the new ideas, you need to see them used repeatedly in slightly different situations, and this is what you find here. The examples are written so that you proceed in small steps, reinforcing what you already know and always adding a little bit of new information or perspective.

- The multitude of examples allows me to go quite deep into the subject even while staying at the beginner level. Many starter books show a new notion through one or two textbook examples and move on. This is not so here. The examples chosen stem from real programming. They often represent the core of various situations I have found myself in when developing real-world software. I cover the core topics distilled to an elementary level.

- I have authored several programming books in the Czech language and have found that many readers preferred the coding examples over the explanatory text. This probably reflects our modern times of information overload. That is why I have written this book using a concise, task-oriented approach. You will find a minimum of talking and a maximum of action here. Enjoy it!

# How to Work with the Book

Before I start telling you how to prepare your computer, here are some tips on how you might work with the book to get maximum usefulness out of it:

- The book contains many exercises. These are not tasks for practicing what you have already learned. These tasks constitute the main instructions of the book. This means you are not supposed to try to *solve* them after reading what the task is. What you are supposed to do is to read what the task is about, see its illustrative screenshots, and go immediately to study its solution.

- You should not just *read* the solutions. You are strongly encouraged to type them on your computer and get them working. The exercises will have much greater impact on your understanding if you try everything yourself.

- In case you cannot get some exercise working, you can always check the accompanying source codes at `https://github.com/apress/charp-programming-for-absolute-begs`. Also, you might want to visit my website at `http://moderniprogramovani.cz/en/`.

- In each task, try to understand the logic of its solution. Also, it is helpful to try your own modifications of the tasks. Do not be afraid to play with the code. It is not a chemical lab; you will not blow up your house!

- I have included lots of comments in the solutions. Actually, each logical part of the code is prepended by a blank line and a comment explaining its purpose. Please pay close attention to these comments; they are the primary hints situated exactly in the places they are explaining. Only the longer explanations I have placed outside of the code, into the regular text of the book.

- At the end of each chapter, you can relax and read its summary. You can then compare it to what you learned about the topics covered before moving on to the next chapter.

# What to Install on Your Computer

That's enough introduction. Let's proceed to how to get ready—or, rather, how you should get your computer ready.

## Development Environment

To work with this book, you need a single program installed on your computer—a so-called integrated development environment (IDE).

What is an IDE? Well, to perform any activity on a computer, you need the appropriate software. To write text, you use a word processor; to view a web page, you use a browser; and so on. In the same way, to create programs, you use specialized software that facilitates programming, and this software is the development environment. In other words, it is a "program for programming."

It is often called an "integrated" development environment because it brings together all the programmer's activities—writing the code using smart editor, building the program into a computer-ready form, launching and testing it, peeking into computer's memory, and so on—into one place with tools to help.

## Visual Studio

For C#, the number-one development environment is Visual Studio. At the time of writing, the latest version is 2017, and it is available in a free-of-charge edition called Community (see Figure 1-1). This is what I will use throughout the book, and in a minute you are going to learn how to install it.

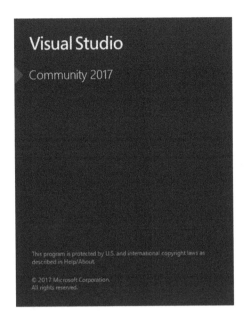

***Figure 1-1.*** *Visual Studio Community*

# Windows Versions

Visual Studio requires the Windows operating system. If you perform a web search for *Visual Studio system requirements*, you will find the Windows versions supported (see Figure 1-2).

## Visual Studio 2017 System Requirements

| | |
|---|---|
| **Supported Operating Systems** | Visual Studio 2017 will install and run on the following operating systems:<br><br>• Windows 10 version 1507 or higher: Home, Professional, Education, and Enterprise (LTSB and S are not supported)<br>• Windows Server 2016: Standard and Datacenter<br>• Windows 8.1 (with Update 2919355): Core, Professional, and Enterprise<br>• Windows Server 2012 R2 (with Update 2919355): Essentials, Standard, Datacenter<br>• Windows 7 SP1 (with latest Windows Updates): Home Premium, Professional, Enterprise, Ultimate |

***Figure 1-2.*** *Windows versions supported*

As you can see, you do not need to have the latest and greatest version of Windows. As of August 2017, you can even have Windows 7 with Service Pack 1 installed.

## Non-Windows Operating Systems

If you do not have the Windows operating system on your computer, you will be happy to hear about the Visual Studio Code development environment. This is a free-of-charge, multiplatform IDE running also on Linux or Mac, allowing you to program in C# on these systems.

In this book's examples, I will use Visual Studio Community 2017 installed on Windows. I recommend you do the same. If this is not feasible for you, use Visual Studio Code, taking into account that some things might be a little different from what you see in the book.

## Installation

Now you know what to install—Visual Studio Community 2017—so, please, go ahead! Point your web browser to `http://visualstudio.com` and look for something like "Download Community 2017" on the page. Click the button or link, and the installer starts downloading.

During installation, a screen with the different components you can select appears (see Figure 1-3).

***Figure 1-3.*** *Installing Visual Studio*

Be sure to select ".NET desktop development" and click the Install button. After that, the installation should run smoothly.

# Free Registration

After you have installed Visual Studio, you should register your copy (free of charge) the first time you launch it. On the appropriate screen, click the "Sign in" button and enter your Microsoft account credentials. If you do not have a Microsoft account yet, just click the "Sign up" link to get one (see Figure 1-4).

**Figure 1-4.**  *Registrating your copy of Visual Studio*

If you skip this step during the first launch of Visual Studio, you can register later by selecting Help ➤ Register Product in Visual Studio.

# Summary

In this book, you are going to study programming and, specifically, the C# programming language. You will learn to code in C# via many practical exercises that will guide you toward more and more complex topics. To be able to follow along with the exercises, you should prepare your computer in the following ways:

- You need a computer with the Windows operating system (at least Windows 7 with Service Pack 1).

- You need to install an appropriate development environment. In this book, I will work with the free Visual Studio Community 2017.

# PART I

# Data

# CHAPTER 2

# Your First Program

You have your computer ready now, so let's start programming! In this chapter, you will create your first program in the C# language and learn all the steps that you need to perform to do this.

## Seeing It in Action

In this chapter, you'll create a program that displays message "I am starting to program in C#." to the user (see Figure 2-1).

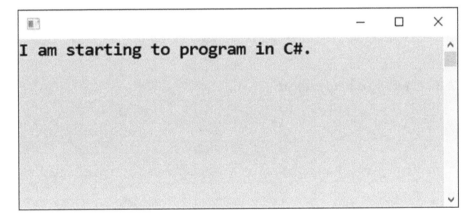

**Figure 2-1.** *Your first program*

## Creating the Project

You start every new program by creating a new project, so let's do that now.

© Radek Vystavěl 2017
R. Vystavěl, *C# Programming for Absolute Beginners*, https://doi.org/10.1007/978-1-4842-3318-4_2

# Launching Visual Studio

Launch Visual Studio and choose File ➤ New ➤ Project from its menu (see Figure 2-2).

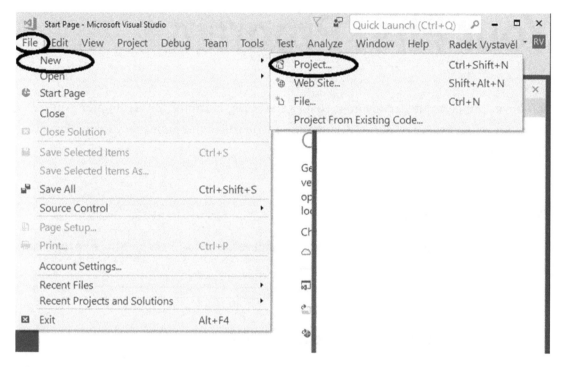

***Figure 2-2.***  *Creating a new project*

The New Project dialog appears (see Figure 2-3).

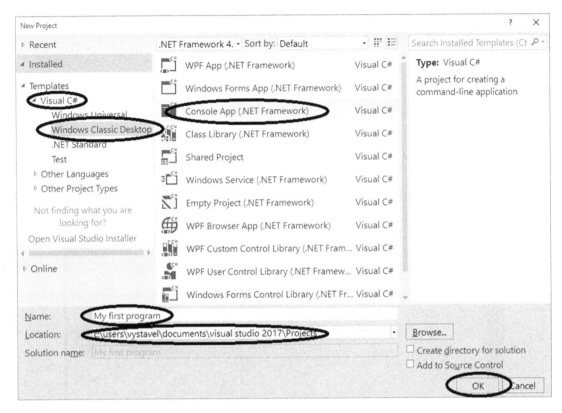

**Figure 2-3.** *New Project dialog*

# Working with the New Project Dialog

In the dialog, follow the steps:

1. On the left, in the Templates section, choose the correct programing language, Visual C#.

2. Expand the Windows Classic Desktop template group.

3. In the middle, choose the Console App template.

4. In the field Name, name your project. For this example, enter **My first program**.

5. In the field Location, check where the project will be placed on your disk.

6. Confirm everything by click the OK button.

# Writing the Program Code

The most important step is writing the program's code, so read on.

## The Look of the Development Environment

After project creation, Visual Studio looks like Figure 2-4.

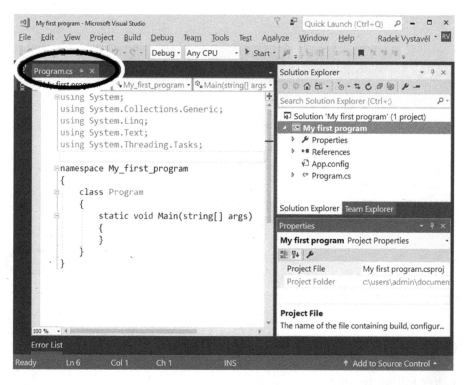

***Figure 2-4.*** *The source code editor in Visual Studio*

The main part of the development environment window is occupied by the *source code editor*. In it, the Program.cs file is opened, as is suggested by the tab's title. Program.cs is the main file of your new project. As you can see, it already contains some source code.

You might wonder where this code came from. You haven't written any line of code yet! The answer is that Visual Studio generated the code when you selected the Console Application template. As you saw when creating the project, Visual Studio contains many different templates; these templates are ready-made project skeletons for different types of programs.

14

You can see that the code contains some strange words like `using`, `namespace`, `class`, and so on. I am not going to explain these now because you do not need a detailed understanding of them at this time. But Visual Studio needs these lines, so just leave them alone. What you do need to know is where to write your own statements, which is what I will explain next.

## Knowing Where to Write Statements

You write program statements between the curly brackets that you find after the line containing the word `Main` (see Figure 2-5).

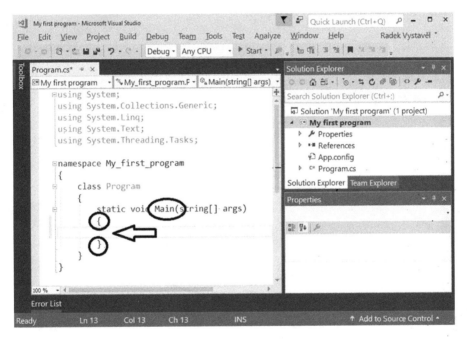

***Figure 2-5.*** *Where you write your statements*

# Writing the Code

In this case, type the following statements **between curly brackets after the Main line**. Make sure to type them **exactly as you see here**. Differences between lowercase and uppercase matter, and semicolons matter, too!

```
// Output of text to the user
Console.WriteLine("I am starting to program in C#.");

// Waiting for Enter
Console.ReadLine();
```

Visual Studio now looks like Figure 2-6.

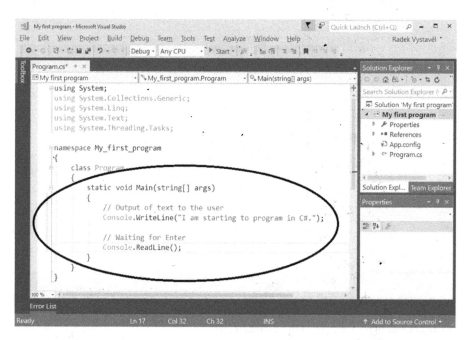

***Figure 2-6.*** *Entering your first code statements*

Please double-check that you typed the statements in the same place as I did. Again, they have to be between the brackets. Also, be careful of the brackets. Do not accidentally delete any of them.

The source code of `Program.cs` now looks like this:

```
using System;
using System.Collections.Generic;
using System.Linq;
using System.Text;
using System.Threading.Tasks;

namespace My_first_program
{
    class Program
    {
        static void Main(string[] args)
        {
            // Output of text to the user
            Console.WriteLine("I am starting to program in C#.");

            // Waiting for Enter
            Console.ReadLine();
        }
    }
}
```

# Understanding Your First Statements

What do these statements do?

- `Console.WriteLine` outputs (writes) a single line to the user.

- `Console.ReadLine`, in general, reads a line of text that the user enters with the keyboard. In this case, however, the purpose of the statement is to make your program wait for the user to press Enter when everything is done. In other words, you do not want the program window to disappear immediately.

- Everything following the two slashes (//) until the end of a corresponding line is ignored. This text contains your remarks. Visual Studio colors them in green.

## Using IntelliSense

You probably have noticed that when you type, Visual Studio offers you available possibilities (see Figure 2-7). You can choose an option either using the mouse or using the arrow keys followed by pressing the Tab key.

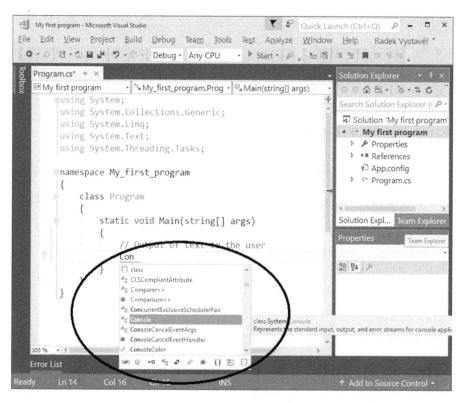

***Figure 2-7.*** *Using IntelliSense*

The part of Visual Studio that provides you with these hints is called IntelliSense. Get used to relying on it as much as you can. It is the best way to avoid unnecessary typos.

## Saving the Project

You have written several lines of code, so you probably want to save them. According to the default settings of Visual Studio, projects are automatically saved before every program launch. However, sometimes you want to save the changes manually. In that case, choose File ➤ Save All from the Visual Studio menu.

# Launching Your Program

Having written your program, you usually want to *launch* it to see it "in action" and to check whether it does what you meant it to do.

Prepare yourself. The great moment of your first program launch is coming! Choose Debug ➤ Start Debugging from the Visual Studio menu, or just press the F5 key.

Visual Studio builds and launches your program (see Figure 2-8). The program outputs the specified text and waits for the Enter key to be pressed, which is exactly the way you have programmed it.

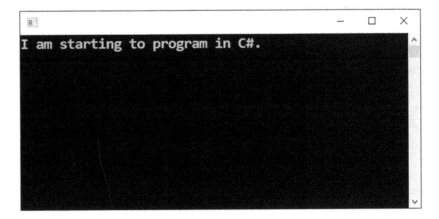

***Figure 2-8.*** *Launching your program*

Now in the role of the user, press the Enter key. The program terminates, and the "black window" disappears.

# Note

With the default settings of your computer, your programs will appear with white type on a black background, as you can see in Figure 2-8. However, for better readability, I will show all the later screenshots in black type on a light background. Actually, I have already done this at the beginning of this chapter.

# Changing Text Size

Do you think the outputted text is too small? Do you need to enlarge the font your programs will use?

If so, click the title bar icon at the upper-left corner of the "black screen" of the launched program and choose Defaults (see Figure 2-9).

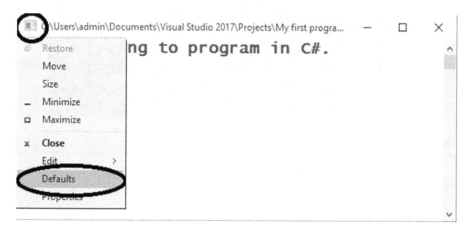

*Figure 2-9.* *Choosing Defaults*

Then click the Font tab, change the font according to your preferences, and confirm the change by clicking the OK button (see Figure 2-10).

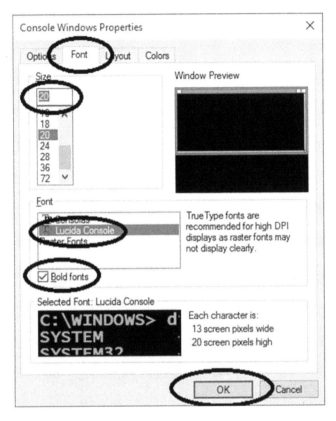

***Figure 2-10.*** *Changing the font*

When the next program launches, the new font will be used.

# Dealing with Errors

If you did not write the statements exactly the way I showed you or you wrote them in the wrong place, program build will terminate unsuccessfully with errors.

Let's try this! Delete the semicolon at the end of the line with the Console.WriteLine statement.

When you try to launch your program (by pressing the F5 key), the trial terminates with an error dialog (see Figure 2-11).

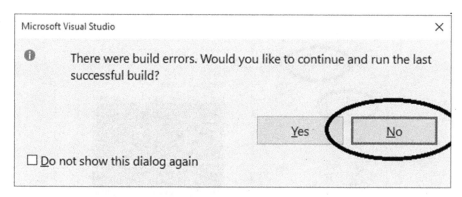

***Figure 2-11.*** *Getting an error*

In this dialog, **always click No**; you do not want to run some older version of your program (if it exists).

After clicking No, the Error List pane appears (see Figure 2-12).

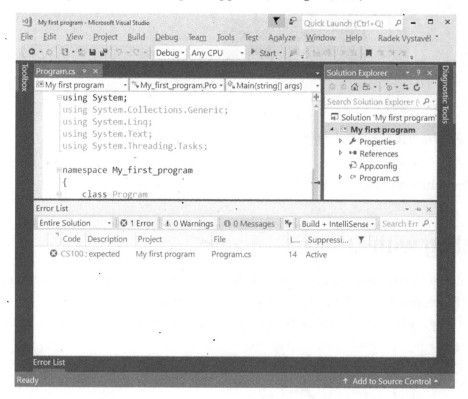

***Figure 2-12.*** *Error list*

Return the deleted semicolon, and everything will be fine again. In the future, it may be more difficult to find what you did wrong, especially at the beginning of your programming career. That's OK—my opinion is that you can't become an expert in a field until you have made all the possible mistakes there are.

# Finishing Your Work

You have just gone through all the essential steps of program development. You will proceed along the same lines in every future project you do.

You now need to learn how to terminate your work and how to get back to it later. The former is simple; you can finish your work on this project by choosing File ➤ Close Solution from the menu or by closing the whole Visual Studio program.

# Restoring Your Work

When you want to get back to your project later, you can reopen it in Visual Studio using one of the following ways:

- *From the Start Page*: This is the page that appears immediately after Visual Studio starts and contains links to your recent projects (see Figure 2-13). Simply click the right one.

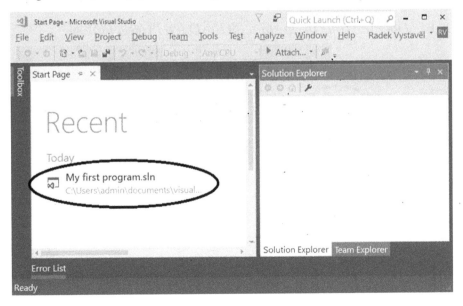

***Figure 2-13.***  *Using the Start Page*

- *From the Open Project dialog*: Select File ➤ Open ➤ Project/Solution from the menu. The Open Project dialog appears in which you should locate your project (see Figure 2-14). Specifically, look for files with the `.sln` extension. If you cannot see the file extensions, turn their display on in Windows File Explorer (on the View tab, select the "File name extensions" check box), as shown in Figure 2-15.

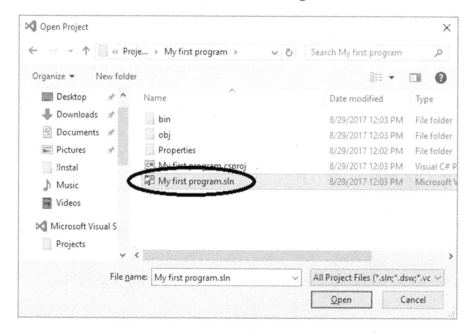

***Figure 2-14.*** *Opening your program with the Open Project dialog*

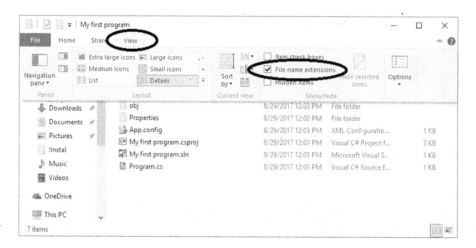

***Figure 2-15.*** *Showing extensions*

- *From the File menu*: Select File ➤ Recent Projects and Solutions.
  Visual Studio remembers what project you were working on recently.
  Just choose the appropriate project (see Figure 2-16).

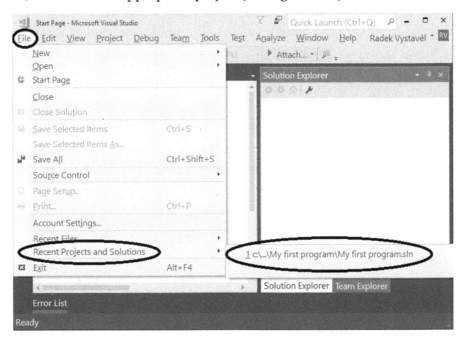

***Figure 2-16.*** *Opening your program from the File menu*

# Transferring Your Work

You may also be interested in how to transfer your program to somewhere else from your computer. There are actually two questions in this matter. First, how do you transfer it so you can work on it later on a different computer, and second, how do you transfer it to other people to use it?

# Transferring the Project

Do you want to transfer your project so you can work on it on another computer? If you're using a flash drive, OneDrive, or something similar, just transfer its whole folder.

## Transferring the Program to Others

Do you want other people to use your program? Simply hand them a copy of the file with the extension .exe that you can find in the bin\debug subfolder of your project (e.g., My first program.exe). They can directly run the file; they do not need either the whole project or Visual Studio.

## Using Solution Explorer

There is an important issue with transferring your projects onto another computer that you should be familiar with. Sometimes a project is opened without a source code editor (see Figure 2-17).

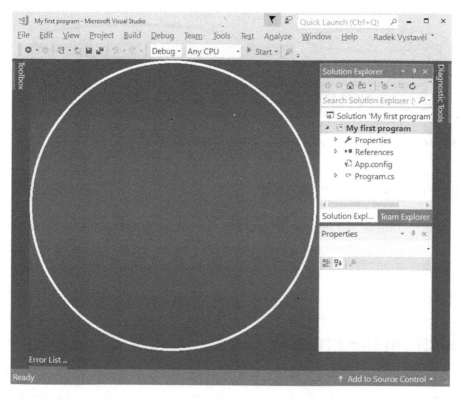

*Figure 2-17.* *Opening a project without a source code editor*

What do you do in such a situation? There is a pane (subwindow) called Solution Explorer usually located at the right side of the Visual Studio window. Simply double-click your source code file, `Program.cs` (see Figure 2-18).

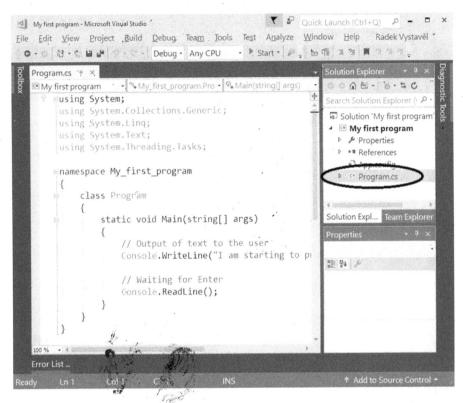

***Figure 2-18.*** *Opening your source code via Solution Explorer*

Did Solution Explorer disappear? No problem! At any time, you can display it using the menu selection View ➤ Solution Explorer (see Figure 2-19).

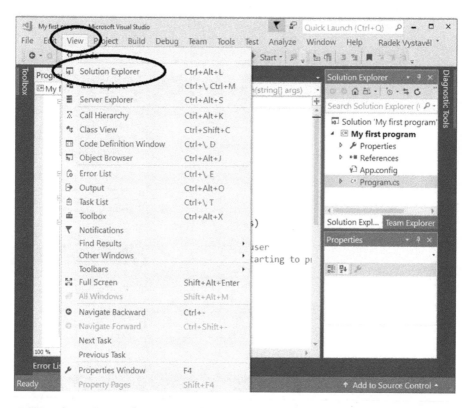

***Figure 2-19.***  *Opening Solution Explorer*

# Summary

In this chapter, you made your first program, and you also started learning about how to work with the Visual Studio development environment. You went through all the steps of program development, which essentially are these:

- Creating the project

- Editing the source code

- Saving the source code

- Launching the program

- Detecting and removing possible errors

You also learned how to transfer your program to other computers. Specifically, you studied the following:

- How to transfer your project onto another computer of yours to work on it elsewhere

- How to deploy your program to your users

# CHAPTER 3

# Dealing with Output

You already know all the main steps that you should take when developing a program in the C# language. In addition, you have already seen the important statement `Console.WriteLine`, which displays data on your user's screen. In this chapter, you will extend your knowledge of this statement. I will also show you other possibilities for the output.

## Producing Numeric Output

You already know how to display some text. In this section, you will learn how to display a number.

## Task

You will write a program that displays the number 37 (see Figure 3-1).

*Figure 3-1.* *The program in action*

© Radek Vystavěl 2017
R. Vystavěl, *C# Programming for Absolute Beginners*, https://doi.org/10.1007/978-1-4842-3318-4_3

# Solution

In Visual Studio, create new project called Numeric Output. The code is similar to the previous program you wrote in Chapter 2, as shown here:

```
static void Main(string[] args)
{
    // Output of a number to the user
    Console.WriteLine(37);

    // Waiting for Enter
    Console.ReadLine();
}
```

---

**Note**   In this example, and all the following examples in the book, I show you just the block of code after the line with the `Main` word. This is the block of code you are in control of; in other words, it's the block of code you change. The rest of the `Program.cs` source code should remain intact the same way you left it in your first program from the previous chapter.

---

To be sure you understand me, the whole source code looks like this:

```
using System;
using System.Collections.Generic;
using System.Linq;
using System.Text;
using System.Threading.Tasks;

namespace Numeric_output
{
    class Program
    {
        static void Main(string[] args)
        {
            // Output of a number to the user
            Console.WriteLine(37);
```

```
        // Waiting for Enter
        Console.ReadLine();
    }
  }
}
```

But, again, this is the last time you will see the whole source code. There is no need to repeat the Visual Studio–generated code each time I show an example because you will never change it. If you are ever in doubt, you can consult the complete sample projects accompanying the book.

After typing in the code, launch the program using the F5 key. To terminate the program, press Enter.

## Discussion

Unlike with text, you do not surround numbers with quotes.

Of course, you could surround "37" in quotes, but there is a profound difference between the number 37 and the text "37"—you can calculate with numbers. That is why you are learning now how to work with numbers correctly.

## Making Calculations

The next task is to make a simple calculation.

# Task

You are going to display to the user what 1 plus 1 is (see Figure 3-2).

**Figure 3-2.**  *1 plus 1*

# Solution

Here is the code:

```
static void Main(string[] args)
{
    // Output of a calculation
    Console.WriteLine(1 + 1);

    // Waiting for Enter
    Console.ReadLine();
}
```

Type it in and launch the program!

# Note

In programming, this kind of calculation (generally, a combination of values) is called an *expression.*

# Making More Complex Calculations

Of course, you do not need a computer to add 1 to 1. But what about 1 plus 2 times 3? Do you think this is ridiculously trivial again? Wait just a minute because even in this simple case mistakes are easy to make!

## Task

You'll create a program to add 1 plus 2 times 3.

## Solution

Here is the code:

```
static void Main(string[] args)
{
    // Multiplication has greater priority
    Console.WriteLine(1 + 2*3);

    // Forcing priority using parentheses
    Console.WriteLine((1 + 2)*3);

    // Waiting for Enter
    Console.ReadLine();
}
```

The launched program looks like Figure 3-3.

***Figure 3-3.***  *Doing more complex calculations*

## Discussion

Note the following about this program:

- The purpose of this task was to show you that you always have to know what exactly needs to be calculated. In this example, you have to make up your mind about whether you want to do addition first or multiplication first.

- In basic math rules, multiplication and division have higher priority than addition or subtraction. It is the same in programming as in mathematics. If you first want to add 1 to 2 and then multiply by 3, you need to use parentheses around the 1 and 2.

- I have not used spaces around the multiplication symbol (asterisk), but this has nothing to do with the calculation order. It just looks better to me. In C#, spaces and line breaks do not matter. (Of course, you should not break a word in the middle.)

- Finally, the example shows that the computer executes program statements in the order they are written. This means from the top down.

## Joining Text

You will now explore that the plus operator (+) can be used also with text, not just with numbers. In other words, it adds text together.

# Task

The task is to explore how to add text together (see Figure 3-4).

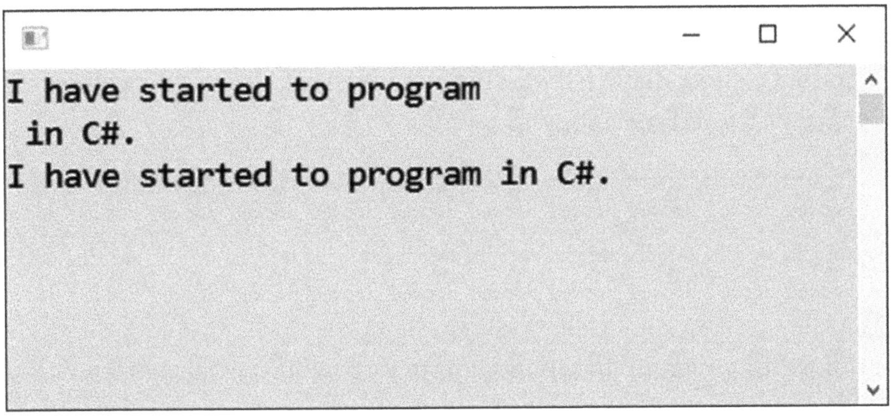

**Figure 3-4.** *Joining text*

# Solution

Here is the code:

```
static void Main(string[] args)
{
    // Normal text
    Console.WriteLine("I have started to program");

    // Also normal text
    Console.WriteLine(" in C#.");

    // Joining two texts using plus sign
    Console.WriteLine("I have started to program" + " in C#.");

    // Waiting for Enter
    Console.ReadLine();
}
```

Note the space before the *in* preposition!

# Outputting Special Characters

Sometimes you need to output a special character to the screen. Here are some examples:

- Output Enter to terminate a line.

- Output a quote mark. (Quotes in C# serve as text delimiters, so they must be treated specially.)

- Output a Unicode character (of course, if your font knows how to draw it).

## Task

Now you will write a program that shows how to work with special characters.

## Solution

To work with special characters, you use *escape sequences*. In C#, an escape sequence starts with a backslash.

```
static void Main(string[] args)
{
    // Multiline output
    Console.WriteLine("First line\r\nSecond line");

    // I prefer specifying "Enter" in more human form
    Console.WriteLine("First line" + Environment.NewLine + "Second line");

    // Text containing a quote
    Console.WriteLine("The letter started so sweet: \"My Darling\"");

    // Unicode characters, in this case Greek beta
    Console.WriteLine("If the font knows, here is Greek beta: \u03B2");
```

```
// Backslashes themselves need to be doubled
Console.WriteLine("Path to desktop on my computer: " + "C:\\Users\\
vystavel\\Desktop");

// Waiting for Enter
Console.ReadLine();
}
```

The result should look like Figure 3-5.

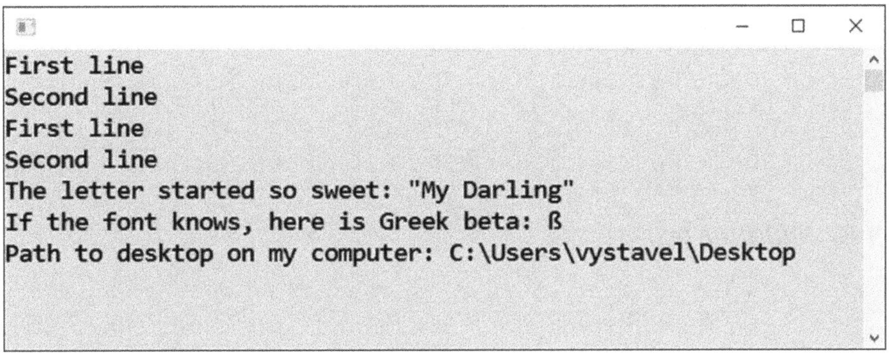

***Figure 3-5.*** *Working with special characters*

## Discussion

Note the following about this program:

- In C#, a backslash in text introduces a so-called escape sequence. But what if you want to output a backslash? Then you need to double it. This is often the case when dealing with file paths in the Windows operating system.

- Console applications will recognize even the simple \n as a line terminator (meaning Enter). However, in many other C# programs, you need "the whole Enter," which is signified with \r\n. That is why you used it in this program. You also used Environment.NewLine, which is definitely the best alternative since it is nicely human readable.

# Using Preformatted Text

Sometimes you might want to display multiline text in one go (see Figure 3-6).

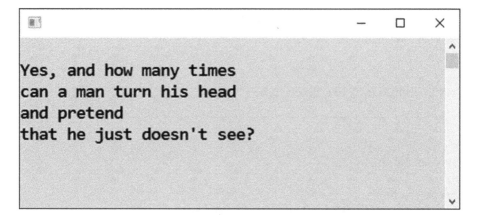

**Figure 3-6.** *Multiline text*

# Task

You will create a program to display multiline text.

# Solution

You prepend the opening quote mark of the text with the at (@) sign, as shown here:

```
static void Main(string[] args)
{
    // Bob Dylan...
    Console.WriteLine(@"
Yes, and how many times
can a man turn his head
and pretend
that he just doesn't see?
");

    // Waiting for Enter
    Console.ReadLine();
}
```

## Note

The at (@) sign also switches off escape sequences. That is why you might find it useful when dealing with file paths in Windows (mentioned earlier); in that case, you do not have to double each backslash.

# Adding 1 and 1

In the next task, you will return to the problem of adding 1 to 1. Are you wondering why I am returning to such a trivial task? Well, even doing something as simple as adding 1 to 1 can go wrong. Let's see.

## Task

The task is to explore different ways of putting two numbers together (see Figure 3-7).

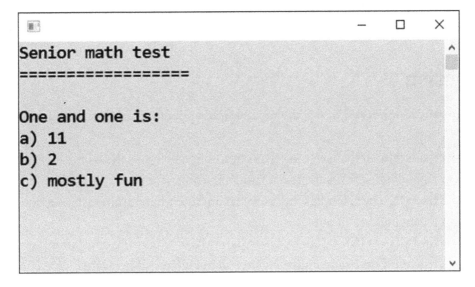

*Figure 3-7.* *Putting numbers together*

# Solution

Here is the code:

```
static void Main(string[] args)
{
    // Pay special attention when mixing texts with numbers!
    Console.WriteLine(
@"Senior math test

==================

One and one is:");
    Console.WriteLine("a) " + 1 + 1);
    Console.WriteLine("b) " + (1 + 1));
    Console.WriteLine("c) " + "mostly fun");

    // Waiting for Enter
    Console.ReadLine();
}
```

# Discussion

When you mix numbers with text, the result might appear different from what you expect!

Let's consider the first answer (a). The computer calculates the whole expression from left to right. First, it takes the text a) and a number (the first 1). It joins them together to be a) 1. Then, it takes this new text and the final number (the second 1) and again joins them together to obtain the text a) 11.

The second answer (b) is different. The parentheses make the computer perform the addition of the numbers first, joining the text on the left only afterward.

Sometimes it may be more transparent to precalculate the intermediate results and store them in variables. This is what you are going to study in the next chapter. Of course, variables have many more uses than this, as you are going to see.

# Summary

In this chapter, you explored several possibilities that the `Console.WriteLine` statement gives you for different kinds of output. Specifically, you have learned the following:

- In addition to text, you can work with numbers in your programs. Unlike with text, you do not surround numbers with quotes.

- You can combine several values into expressions. For this purpose, you use operators such as +, -, and *. With numbers, they do ordinary arithmetic. The plus operator works also with text, in which case it joins two pieces of text into a single one.

- In calculations, you always have to be careful about the order in which the result is evaluated. Multiplication and division have precedence over addition and subtraction. To force a different evaluation order, use parentheses.

- Special characters such as quotes or newlines are output using escape sequences starting with backslash.

- You can conveniently output preformatted multiline text by prepending it with an at (@) sign.

# CHAPTER 4

# Using Variables

In this chapter, you will learn all about variables. A *variable* is a named place in the computer's memory where a program can store something. It can be anything you want. In fact, you can have as many variables in your program as you need.

This chapter will start with some simple examples, but eventually you will see that variables are absolutely fundamental to programming.

## Storing Text

The first task will introduce you to variables. You will learn how to perform some basic operations with them.

## Task

You'll create a variable named message. Afterward, you will store some text in it. Finally, you will display the value of the variable to the user.

## Solution

Here is the code:

```
static void Main(string[] args)
{
    // Declaration of a variable to store text
    string message;

    // Storing a value in prepared variable (assignment statement)
    message = "I can't live with you.";
```

© Radek Vystavěl 2017
R. Vystavěl, *C# Programming for Absolute Beginners*, https://doi.org/10.1007/978-1-4842-3318-4_4

```
    // Another variable (initialized with some value)
    string anotherMessage = "I can't live without you.";

    // Output of variables
    Console.WriteLine(message);
    Console.WriteLine(anotherMessage);

    // Waiting for Enter
    Console.ReadLine();
}
```

# Discussion

Now let's discuss the solution.

## Variable Declaration

If you want to use a variable, you need to *declare* (create) it first.

The general syntax of a variable declaration statement is as follows:
*typeName[space]variableName[semicolon]*.

In this case, it reads as follows:

```
string message;
```

The type denotes the *category of values* that you want to store in the variable. In this case, you want to store text, which is why you used the type called `string`.

## Alternative

There is an alternative way to write a variable declaration statement. In front of the semicolon, you can use an equal sign and the initial value of the variable.

Here is an example of this syntax:

```
string anotherMessage = "I can't live without you.";
```

## Assignment Statement

There is one more thing in the code that needs to be explained. The second statement is as follows:

```
message = "I can't live with you.";
```

This stores a value (the text "I can't live with you.") in the prepared variable (`message`), and it is called an *assignment statement*. You use it whenever you want to store something.

The general syntax of the assignment statement is as follows:

*WHERE (TO STORE) = WHAT (TO STORE);*

# Storing Numbers

In the next task, you will learn about variables that store numbers rather than text.

# Task

You will create (*declare*) a variable called `number`. Afterward, you will store some number in it. Finally, you will display the variable's value to the user.

# Solution

The data type for numeric values is called `int`. Strictly speaking, this is the data type for *whole* numbers (integers). It will not be long until you see that distinguishing whole and decimal numbers matters in programming.

```
static void Main(string[] args)
{
    // Variable for storing number (with initial value)
    int number = -12;

    // Output of value of the variable
    Console.WriteLine("Value of the variable: " + number);

    // Waiting for Enter
    Console.ReadLine();
}
```

Do not forget, numbers are entered *without quotes*.

# Adding 1 and 1

What? Adding 1 and 1 again? You probably think I'm going mad!

## Task

In the previous chapter, I told you that variables could provide you with greater certainty when combining numbers with text. Now I am returning to that suggestion.

## Solution

Here is the code:

```
static void Main(string[] args)
    {
        // Precalculation of result (into a variable)
        int sum = 1 + 1;

        // Output to the user
        Console.WriteLine(
@"Answer to Senior math test
==========================

One and one is: " + sum);

        // Waiting for Enter
        Console.ReadLine();
    }
}
```

For the result of running the program, see Figure 4-1.

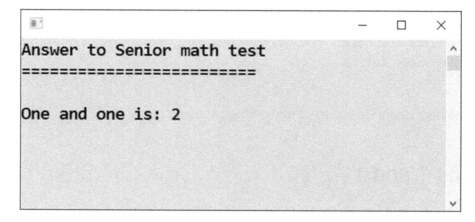

***Figure 4-1.*** *The result of the 1 plus 1 program*

## Discussion

Please compare the calculation of adding 1 to 1 to the calculations from the previous chapter. Here you explicitly store the result in a variable. This allows you to avoid possible problems with the order of evaluation and getting the incorrect answer of 11.

# Doing Calculations with Variables

In the next task, you will learn how to use several variables at once.

## Task

You are going to store some numbers in two variables. After that, you will calculate their sum into the third one.

## Solution

Here is the code:

```
static void Main(string[] args)
{
    // 1. SOLUTION
    // Values to be summed
    int firstNumber = 42;
    int secondNumber = 11;

    // Calculating
    int sum = firstNumber + secondNumber;

    // Output
    Console.WriteLine("Sum is: " + sum);

    // 2. SOLUTION
    // Declaring all variables at once
    int thirdNumber, fourthNumber, newSum;
```

```
    // Values to be summed
    thirdNumber = 42;
    fourthNumber = 11;

    // Calculating
    newSum = thirdNumber + fourthNumber;

    // Output
    Console.WriteLine("Calculated another way: " + newSum);

    // Waiting for Enter
    Console.ReadLine();
}
```

## Discussion

The two (alternative) solutions show two cases you will often meet.

- You declare a variable and *immediately* store a value in it.

- You declare a variable first and store a value in it *later*.

# Assembling a Grand Combination

Often you need to assemble your output from several values. In this task, you will learn how.

## Task

I will show you how to assemble complex text via an example of a soccer match result (Figure 4-2).

*Figure 4-2.* *Grand combination program*

In the example, you have some fixed text, some (potentially) variable text, and some (potentially) variable numbers. This is a typical real-world situation.

## Solution

To store (potentially) variable values, you use variables. Of course, the values are actually fixed in this simple program, but generally you would be getting them from somewhere else (such as a user, file, database, or web service). You will learn later in the book how to get input from a user.

```
static void Main(string[] args)
{
    // Data in variables
    string club1 = "FC Liverpool";
    string club2 = "Manchester United";
    int goals1 = 3;
    int goals2 = 2;

    // Output of match result
    Console.WriteLine(
        "Match " + club1 + " - " + club2 +
        " ended with result " +
        goals1 + ":" + goals2 + ".");

    // Waiting for Enter
    Console.ReadLine();
}
```

## Discussion

In the solution, you should especially note the following:

- You are using variables with different data types to store different kinds of values.

- You are constructing the displayed message from nine parts joined together by eigth plus signs. Some of the parts of the message are fixed, while the others are variable.

# Working with Decimal Numbers

In programming, you need to thoroughly distinguish between whole and decimal numbers. You already know how to work with whole numbers, so now you will look at the decimals.

## Task

In this task, I will show you some examples of how to work with decimals.

## Solution

In C#, there is a type called double for decimal numbers. Here is the code:

```
static void Main(string[] args)
{
    // IN CODE, decimal separator is always DOT regardless of computer
    language settings
    double piApproximately = 3.14;

    // Pi is already available in C#
    double piMorePrecisely = Math.PI;

    // Decimal numbers have always limited precision
    double notCompletelyOne = 0.999999999999999999;

    // Outputs
    Console.WriteLine("Pi value from our code: " + piApproximately);
    Console.WriteLine("Pi value from C#: " + piMorePrecisely);
    Console.WriteLine("This should not be exact one: " + notCompletelyOne);

    // Waiting for Enter
    Console.ReadLine();
}
```

## Discussion

Please note the following:

- In code, you always need to use a decimal *point* as a separator between the integer and decimal parts of a number.

- However, the output depends on your Windows settings. As you can see in Figure 4-3, the output on my computer uses a comma as a decimal separator since I have my computer set to the Czech language.

- You can also see that decimal numbers do not have infinite precision. They are rounded after approximately 15 significant digits.

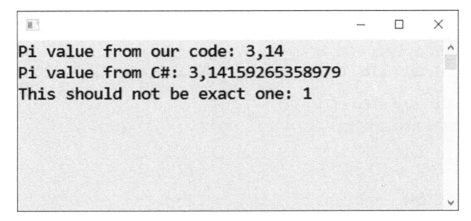

*Figure 4-3.* *The result of the decimal numbers program*

# Working with Logical Values

In programming, you often work with *logical values*, which are the values of "yes" and "no."

# Task

In this task, I will show you how to work with logical values.

# Solution

The type for logical values is called bool in C#. The value "yes" is written as true, and the value "no" is written as false. Here is the code:

```
static void Main(string[] args)
{
    // Two logical (Boolean) variables
    bool thePrettiestGirlLovesMe = true;
    bool iAmHungry = false;

    // Use exclamation mark to negate logical value
    bool iAmNotHungry = !iAmHungry;

    // Output
    Console.WriteLine("She loves me: " + thePrettiestGirlLovesMe);
    Console.WriteLine("I am hungry: " + iAmHungry);
    Console.WriteLine("I am not hungry: " + iAmNotHungry);

    // Waiting for Enter
    Console.ReadLine();
}
```

# Discussion

Note that you use an exclamation mark whenever you need to negate a logical value (to flip it from "yes" to "no" and back again).

# Summary

In this chapter, you were introduced to the important concept of variables. In every real program, you need to temporarily store values (calculation results, user inputs, etc.) in a computer's memory, and this is exactly what you use variables for. A variable is a place in memory that has a name to reference it and its data type to be clear about what kind of data you will store in it.

Specifically, you learned the following:

- Before you can use a variable, you must declare it. An appropriate statement is `string message;`.

- To store a value in a variable, you use the assignment statement format of *where = what;*. An example is `message = "Some text";`.

- In C#, the data type for text is `string`.

- The data type for the whole numbers (integers) is `int`.

- In programming, contrary to common usage, care must be taken to distinguish between whole and decimal numbers.

- The data type for decimal numbers is `double`.

- There is a special data type called `bool` for storing so-called logical values `true` and `false`, which are computer equivalents of "yes" and "no."

# CHAPTER 5

# Working with Objects

Variables of type `string`, `int`, `double`, and `bool` always contain a single value—text, a single number, or a single yes/no value. However, such "atomic" values can be grouped into aggregates that are called *objects*. A single object can contain multiple values that are called its *components* or *members*. Grouping can go so far that an object can contain several other objects inside itself, for example. In this chapter, you are going to learn about objects.

## What Time Is It?

The first object you will encounter is a `DateTime` object containing various components of a single instance of time, such as day, month, year, hour, minute, second, and so on.

## Task

You will write a program that displays the current date and time to the user (see Figure 5-1).

```
Now is 10/6/2017 10:08:16 AM
```

*Figure 5-1.* *Displaying the current date and time*

In this task, you will get know objects of the `DateTime` type.

© Radek Vystavěl 2017
R. Vystavěl, *C# Programming for Absolute Beginners*, https://doi.org/10.1007/978-1-4842-3318-4_5

## Solution

Here is the code:

```
static void Main(string[] args)
{
    // Variable of DateTime type, at first empty
    DateTime now;

    // Storing of current date and time into our variable
    now = DateTime.Now;

    // Output
    Console.WriteLine("Now is " + now);

    // Waiting for Enter
    Console.ReadLine();
}
```

# What Date Is It Today?

Let's go further with the DateTime object.

## Task

Say you are interested only in today's date, with the time component excluded (see Figure 5-2).

***Figure 5-2.*** *Displaying just the date*

The difference between today's date and current time can be substantial in many programs!

## Solution

Here is the code:

```
static void Main(string[] args)
{
    // Variable of DateTime type, at first empty
    DateTime today;

    // Storing of today's date (without time component)
    today = DateTime.Today;

    // Output
    Console.WriteLine("Today is " + today);

    // Waiting for Enter
    Console.ReadLine();
}
```

# Working with Date Components

You might wonder where the mentioned *components* of an object are. Let's see the components of the DateTime object. If you append a variable of the DateTime type with a dot, Visual Studio IntelliSense displays all the possible components available.

## Task

You will learn about the various components of the DateTime object.

## Solution

Here is the code:

```
static void Main(string[] args)
{
    // Current date and time (using single statement)
    DateTime now = DateTime.Now;

    // Picking up individual components
    int day = now.Day;
    int month = now.Month;
    int year = now.Year;
    int hours = now.Hour;
    int minutes = now.Minute;
    int seconds = now.Second;
    DateTime justDateWithoutTime = now.Date;

    // Output
    Console.WriteLine("Day: " + day);
    Console.WriteLine("Month: " + month);
    Console.WriteLine("Year: " + year);
    Console.WriteLine("Hours: " + hours);
    Console.WriteLine("Minutes: " + minutes);
    Console.WriteLine("Seconds: " + seconds);
    Console.WriteLine("Date component: " + justDateWithoutTime);
```

```
    // Formatting output our way
    Console.WriteLine("Our output: " +
        year + ", " + month + "/" + day +
        " " +
        hours + " hours " + minutes + " minutes");

    // Waiting for Enter
    Console.ReadLine();
}
```

Figure 5-3 shows the components of the DateTime object.

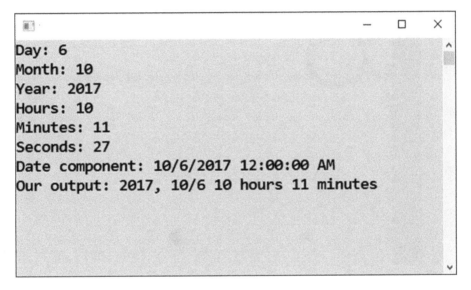

***Figure 5-3.*** *Components of the DateTime object*

# Using Namespaces

Well, now that you have met your first object, I should tell you something about namespaces.

# Important using

With the last project still open, use two slashes to comment out the first line (using System;) in the Program.cs source code (see Figure 5-4). You can also just delete the line. However, to return to the original version, it is more convenient just to comment the line out.

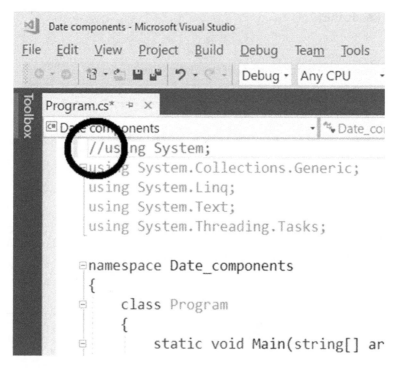

*Figure 5-4.* *Commenting out the first line*

Within an instant, a multitude of red waves appear in the source code. When you try to launch your program using the F5 key, it will not launch (see Figure 5-5).

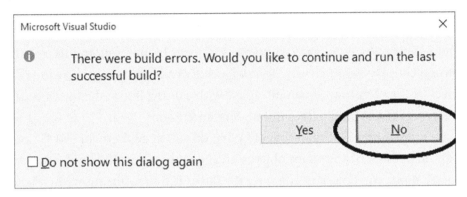

***Figure 5-5.*** *Getting errors*

Just to remind you, always click No in the error dialog that appears.

The Error List pane that appears shows plenty of errors—suddenly Visual Studio "does not know" either DateTime or Console (see Figure 5-6).

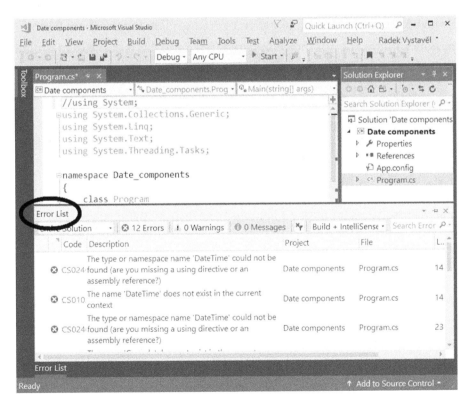

***Figure 5-6.*** *Error List pane*

The `using` line is quite important, isn't it? I am going to explain why next.

# Namespaces

Almost everything in C# belongs to some hierarchically higher unit. In this case, both `DateTime` and `Console` belong to the `System` *namespace*. If you want to use them, you have to declare the corresponding namespace with a `using` line at the top of your source code. Otherwise, Visual Studio does not understand them.

Why are there things like namespaces? What do you need them for? Well, there are not an infinite number of names for objects, so you need to specify which one you are using. For example, you do not need to use the `DateTime` class just from Microsoft; you could program your own `DateTime`, or you could buy some wonderful `DateTime` from another programmer. That is why you need a way to distinguish among them. This way is through *namespaces*.

Every object type belongs to some namespace. For example, the `System` namespace is "managed" by Microsoft. If I prepared my own `DateTime`, I might put it in the `RadekVystavěl.Books` namespace.

Well, maybe no one needs to make their own `DateTime`, but there are better examples. For example, the `TextBox` class prepared for text box controls in programs with graphical user interfaces exists in at least four versions from Microsoft.

- For desktop apps in Windows Forms technology

- For desktop apps in WPF technology

- For web apps

- For so-called Universal (touch-oriented) apps

Each of the text boxes mentioned belongs to a separate namespace.

# Without usings

If you now delete the two slashes you used to comment out the `using System;` line, everything will return to a normal state. However, it might be interesting to see how the program appears with no `using` at all, which is what you are going to do next.

In your source code, you need to *qualify* all the occurrences of `DateTime` and `Console` with the appropriate namespace, i.e., `System`. Qualification is technically performed by prepending the namespace to the name being qualified.

```
//using System;
//using System.Collections.Generic;
//using System.Linq;
//using System.Text;
//using System.Threading.Tasks;

namespace Date_components__without_using_
{
    class Program
    {
        static void Main(string[] args)
        {
            // Current date and time (using single statement)
            System.DateTime now = System.DateTime.Now;

            // Picking up individual components
            int day = now.Day;
            int month = now.Month;
            int year = now.Year;
            int hours = now.Hour;
            int minutes = now.Minute;
            int seconds = now.Second;
            System.DateTime justDateWithoutTime = now.Date;

            // Output
            System.Console.WriteLine("Day: " + day);
            System.Console.WriteLine("Month: " + month);
            System.Console.WriteLine("Year: " + year);
            System.Console.WriteLine("Hours: " + hours);
            System.Console.WriteLine("Minutes: " + minutes);
            System.Console.WriteLine("Seconds: " + seconds);
            System.Console.WriteLine("Date component: " +
            justDateWithoutTime);

            // Formatting output our way
            System.Console.WriteLine("Our output: " +
                year + ", " + month + "/" + day +
                " " +
```

```
                  hours + " hours " + minutes + " minutes");

         // Waiting for Enter
         System.Console.ReadLine();
      }
   }
}
```

It is better with usings, isn't it?

# Using the Environment Object

To conclude the chapter, you will take one more look at the Environment object you already know. It is fruitful to look at things from different perspectives.

## Task

The Environment object contains information about a program's "surroundings" (that is, about the computer and the operating system). You already saw the Environment. NewLine component. Now you are going to learn about more components.

## Solution

Here is the code:

```
static void Main(string[] args)
{
    // Displaying components of Environment object
    Console.WriteLine("Device name: " + Environment.MachineName);
    Console.WriteLine("64-bit system: " + Environment.Is64BitOperatingSystem);
    Console.WriteLine("User name: " + Environment.UserName);

    // Waiting for Enter
    Console.ReadLine();
}
```

Contrary to the previous program, I have not extracted object components into variables here. I have used them directly just so you could see another possible way of using them.

# Summary

In this chapter, you got acquainted with objects, which are essentially conglomerates of several components. Contrary to "atomic" (single-valued) types such as `int` or `string`, objects usually contain a number of values.

Specifically, you met the following:

- The `DateTime` object, which can be used to retrieve the current date or time.

- The `Environment` object, which can be used to retrieve information about a program's "surroundings" such as computer names or usernames

You also learned the following:

- The objects can be stored in variables of the appropriate type.

- An object's components can be accessed via so-called *dot notation*. You write the name of an object's variable and append the dot, and a list of available components pops up thanks to Visual Studio IntelliSense.

- Each object type belongs to some namespace. To put it simply, namespaces can be viewed as containers of similar object types.

- An important namespace is the `System` namespace, which contains basic object types such as `DateTime` or `Console`.

- You indicate you want to use a specific namespace with a `using` line at the beginning of the source code.

- If you do not include the appropriate `using` line, you have to fully qualify the type's name. This means you prepend the type's name with the namespace's name and a dot.

# CHAPTER 6

# Using Object Actions

You already know from the previous chapter that an object is a kind of data conglomerate consisting of several "pieces of data." You also know that you can access an object's individual components when you enter the object name, a dot, and the component name. In this chapter, you will find that objects in programming are even more complex. You will learn that besides data components, objects can encapsulate actions that you can perform with the corresponding object. Through several tasks, you will get practice using object actions.

## Displaying the Month in Text

This first task will introduce you to actions that you can perform with DateTime objects.

## Task

You will write a program that will display the current date with the month presented by text rather than by a number (or, generally, in long form), as shown in Figure 6-1.

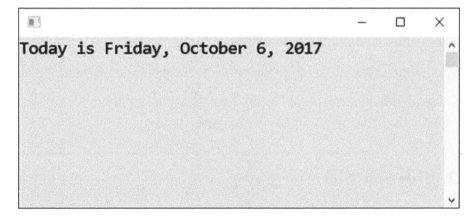

***Figure 6-1.*** *Displaying the current date with the month presented in text*

© Radek Vystavěl 2017
R. Vystavěl, *C# Programming for Absolute Beginners*, https://doi.org/10.1007/978-1-4842-3318-4_6

You can achieve this task using the ToLongDateString action of the DateTime object.

# Solution

Here is the code:

```
static void Main(string[] args)
{
    // Today's date
    DateTime today = DateTime.Today;

    // Output
    Console.WriteLine("Today is " + today.ToLongDateString());

    // Waiting for Enter
    Console.ReadLine();
}
```

# Discussion

Note the following:

- When you launch some object action in C#, the action name is always appended by parentheses (round brackets), even if there is nothing between them.

- The parentheses are often not empty but contain a *parameter* (or parameters), which is some action-specific information. For example, in the case of the Console.WriteLine action, you specify in parentheses what you want to display.

- The actions you can perform with objects are also called *methods*.

- The month name displayed by the ToLongDateString method depends on the operating system language setting.

# Displaying Tomorrow

DateTime objects have more actions available than just converting a date into text. Date arithmetic is especially important.

# Task

You will write a program that displays tomorrow's date (see Figure 6-2).

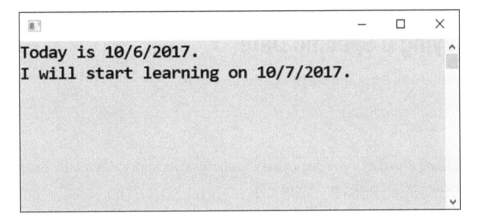

**Figure 6-2.** *Displaying tomorrow's date*

# Solution

DateTime objects can perform further interesting actions (methods), such as the following:

- Using AddDays for date arithmetic
- Using ToShortDateString for displaying the date in short form

Here is the code:

```
static void Main(string[] args)
{
    // Today's date
    DateTime today = DateTime.Today;

    // Tomorrow's date
    DateTime tomorrow = today.AddDays(1);

    // Output
    Console.WriteLine("Today is " + today.ToShortDateString() + ".");
    Console.WriteLine("I will start learning on " + tomorrow.
    ToShortDateString() + ".");
```

```
    // Waiting for Enter
    Console.ReadLine();
}
```

# Displaying a Specific Date

Let's continue with dates and see what a *constructor* is.

## Task

When working with dates, you do not have to always start from today's date. You can choose some specific date (see Figure 6-3).

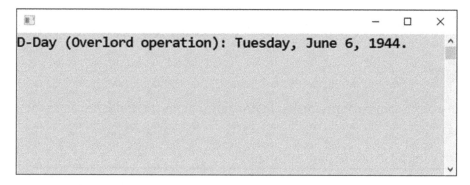

**Figure 6-3.** *Starting with a specific date*

## Solution

You can create a DateTime object initialized with a specific date by calling an object's constructor. You enter the new word, type the name (i.e., DateTime), and use parentheses with the possible parameters. In this case, the parameters are the year, month, and day.

```
static void Main(string[] args)
{
    // A specific date
    DateTime overlordDday = new DateTime(1944, 6, 6);
```

```
    // Output
    Console.WriteLine("D-Day (Overlord operation): " +
                    overlordDday.ToLongDateString() + ".");

    // Waiting for Enter
    Console.ReadLine();
}
```

# Rolling a Single Die

Enough dates. Now you will learn how to work with chance or randomness.

## Task

You will write a program that "throws" a die three times (see Figure 6-4).

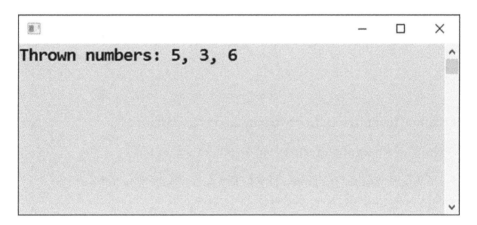

*Figure 6-4.*  *Rolling a die*

## Solution

To work with chance, you need a *random number generator*. In C#, you use the Random object for that purpose.

You first create a Random object by calling its constructor **once** at the beginning of the program run, and afterward you **repeatedly** call its method called Next.

```
static void Main(string[] args)
{
    // Creating random number generator object
    Random randomNumbers = new Random();

    // Repeatedly throwing a die
    int number1 = randomNumbers.Next(1, 6 + 1);
    int number2 = randomNumbers.Next(1, 6 + 1);
    int number3 = randomNumbers.Next(1, 6 + 1);

    // Output
    Console.WriteLine("Thrown numbers: " +
        number1 + ", " +
        number2 + ", " +
        number3);

    // Waiting for Enter
    Console.ReadLine();
}
```

## Note

The Next method (action) requires two parameters in parentheses.

- The lower bound of the interval of generated numbers

- The upper bound **increased by 1** (I'm sorry, but I was not the one who invented this strangeness)

# Rolling Two Dice

Staying with the topic of random numbers, you will now see how to use more than one random number series.

## Task

You will write a program that throws a pair of dice three times (see Figure 6-5). I will show you the right way to do this and the wrong way.

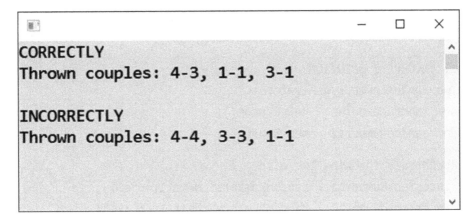

**Figure 6-5.** *Rolling dice three times*

## Solution

The main message of the solution is to use **a single** random number generator. If you had two of them created practically at the same time, they would usually generate **the same numbers**! Here is the code:

```
static void Main(string[] args)
{
    // 1. CORRECT SOLUTION
    // Creating random number generator object
    Random randomNumbers = new Random();

    // Repeatedly throwing two dice
    int correctNumber11 = randomNumbers.Next(1, 6 + 1);
    int correctNumber12 = randomNumbers.Next(1, 6 + 1);

    int correctNumber21 = randomNumbers.Next(1, 6 + 1);
    int correctNumber22 = randomNumbers.Next(1, 6 + 1);

    int correctNumber31 = randomNumbers.Next(1, 6 + 1);
    int correctNumber32 = randomNumbers.Next(1, 6 + 1);

    // Output
    Console.WriteLine("CORRECTLY");
    Console.WriteLine("Thrown couples: " +
        correctNumber11 + "-" + correctNumber12 + ", " +
```

```
            correctNumber21 + "-" + correctNumber22 + ", " +
            correctNumber31 + "-" + correctNumber32);

    // 2. INCORRECT SOLUTION
    // Two random number generators
    Random randomNumbers1 = new Random();
    Random randomNumbers2 = new Random();

    // Repeatedly throwing two dice
    int incorrectNumber11 = randomNumbers1.Next(1, 6 + 1);
    int incorrectNumber12 = randomNumbers2.Next(1, 6 + 1);

    int incorrectNumber21 = randomNumbers1.Next(1, 6 + 1);
    int incorrectNumber22 = randomNumbers2.Next(1, 6 + 1);

    int incorrectNumber31 = randomNumbers1.Next(1, 6 + 1);
    int incorrectNumber32 = randomNumbers2.Next(1, 6 + 1);

    // Output
    Console.WriteLine(); // empty line
    Console.WriteLine("INCORRECTLY");
    Console.WriteLine("Thrown couples: " +
        incorrectNumber11 + "-" + incorrectNumber12 + ", " +
        incorrectNumber21 + "-" + incorrectNumber22 + ", " +
        incorrectNumber31 + "-" + incorrectNumber32);

    // Waiting for Enter
    Console.ReadLine();
}
```

# Getting the Path to the Desktop

To conclude the chapter, you will learn about the actions of yet another object.

# Task

When you work with files, you might want to create a file on the user's desktop. However, everybody has their own file system path to the desktop. I will show you how to find that path (see Figure 6-6).

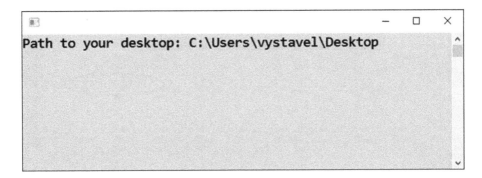

*Figure 6-6.* *Finding the path*

# Solution

You can use your old friend the Environment object. Here is the code:

```
static void Main(string[] args)
{
    // Finding path to the desktop
    string pathToDesktop = Environment.GetFolderPath(Environment.
    SpecialFolder.Desktop);

    // Output
    Console.WriteLine("Path to your desktop: " + pathToDesktop);

    // Waiting for Enter
    Console.ReadLine();
}
```

# Enumeration

Pay special attention to the way you have specified that you are interested in the desktop. The value of Desktop is one of the values of an *enumeration* called Environment.Special Folder.

Whenever Visual Studio wants you to enter an enumeration's value, it usually offers you a corresponding enumeration. In this case, when you choose `GetFolderPath` from IntelliSense and type an open parenthesis afterward, the `Environment.SpecialFolder` enumeration immediately pops up (see Figure 6-7).

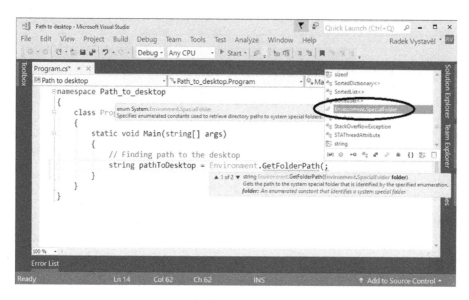

***Figure 6-7.*** *Using IntelliSense*

Select the offered enumeration by using the Tab key, enter a dot, and then select the `Desktop` value.

# Summary

The main purpose of this chapter was to show you that objects are more complex entities than just conglomerates of data components. Specifically, they frequently contain methods, which are actions you can perform that usually operate on the object's data.

You got acquainted with various methods of the DateTime, Random, and Environment objects. Specifically, you studied the following:

- Conversions of dates to text using the ToLongDateString and ToShortDateString methods

- One of the methods for date arithmetic, namely, AddDays

- The Next method for producing a single random number within a specified range

- The GetFolderPath method, which can be used to get the file system path to special folders such as Desktop, Documents, and so on

You also learned about creating objects using constructor calls. You entered the new word, followed by the object type's name and parentheses. Some constructors, like that of Random objects, require just empty parentheses, while others, like that of DateTime, require you to specify some values (year, month, and day) between the parentheses.

Within the final example, you also found usage of so-called enumerations, which are essentially sets of predefined (enumerated) values. Visual Studio's IntelliSense is of great help when working with the enumerations.

# CHAPTER 7

# More About Objects

You have seen an object act as a data conglomerate, or container. You have seen the data it contains as its properties that can be accessed after appending a dot to the object's name. *Accessing* a property means either questioning its value or assigning a new value to it.

You have also discovered that (possibly many) actions can be associated with an object. Actions are called *methods*, and like properties, they can be accessed after appending a dot to the object's name. Moreover, accessing a particular method of an object requires you to add a pair of parentheses to the method's name, with possible parameter values inside them. *Accessing* a method (usually you would say *calling* it) means to launch the operation it implements and to execute the statements it contains inside (without you knowing them).

These are the tenets of programming with objects, the basics of which you studied in the previous two chapters. This chapter will round out your knowledge of objects by exposing you to further insights.

Let's dig into objects a bit more now.

## Text As an Object

In C#, even ordinary text behaves like an object; you can add a dot to text and get plenty of possibilities. Let's take a look.

81

© Radek Vystavěl 2017
R. Vystavěl, *C# Programming for Absolute Beginners*, https://doi.org/10.1007/978-1-4842-3318-4_7

# Task

You will create a program that displays a number of characters of text, converts the text into uppercase, and checks whether the text contains a specific word (Figure 7-1).

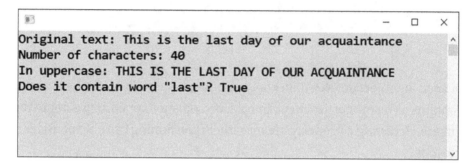

*Figure 7-1.* *The final program*

# Solution

Here is the code:

```
static void Main(string[] args)
{
    // Some text to try things on
    string text = "This is the last day of our acquaintance";

    // What e.g. can be done with texts
    Console.WriteLine("Original text: " + text);
    Console.WriteLine("Number of characters: " + text.Length);
    Console.WriteLine("In uppercase: " + text.ToUpper());
    Console.WriteLine("Does it contain word \"last\"? " + text.
    Contains("last"));

    // Waiting for Enter
    Console.ReadLine();
}
```

# Discussion

Data members (for example, Length) are not accompanied by parentheses, contrary to methods (such as ToUpper, Contains), which always need parentheses even if there is nothing between them.

How can you quickly find out whether something is a method (and therefore will need parentheses)? You can do this either by looking at the violet cube in IntelliSense or looking for parentheses in the tooltip (see Figure 7-2).

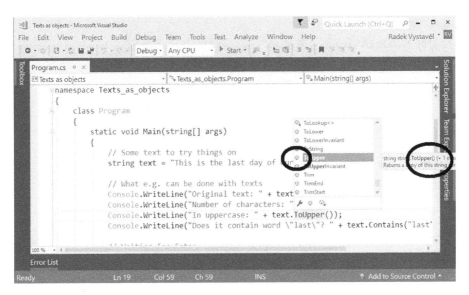

***Figure 7-2.***  *Checking whether something is a method*

# Numbers as Objects

In the previous exercise, you saw that ordinary text—a value of type string—can behave like an object and show internal components such as properties and methods. Now you will see that even numbers can behave like objects, although their actions are much sparser. Actually, the only one worth mentioning is the action of converting to text.

# Task

You will explore what pops up after appending a dot to a numeric variable, and you will learn how to convert from a number to text.

# Solution

To convert a number into its textual representation, use the ToString method. Actually, to convert **anything** into text, you have always the ToString method (action) available in C#.

```
static void Main(string[] args)
{
    // Some number
    int number = 1234;

    // Conversion to text
    //string numberAsText = number; // DOES NOT WORK!
    string numberAsText = number.ToString();

    // Output
    Console.WriteLine("Output of number: " + number);
    Console.WriteLine("Output of text: " + numberAsText);

    // Waiting for Enter
    Console.ReadLine();
}
```

# Discussion

You can see that a value of type int cannot be directly assigned to a variable of type string. You have to convert it to text form first.

Of course, in the output, you cannot see any difference (see Figure 7-3).

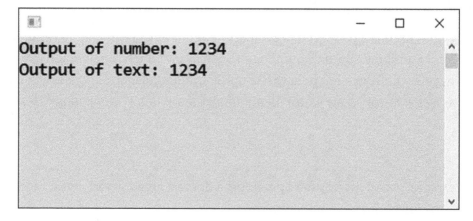

***Figure 7-3.*** *The output*

However, many times you will need to convert a number into text without immediately displaying it. Then you will store the text form of the value in a `string`-typed variable, which is what you have just seen.

To conclude the discussion, I will tell you the reasons why you cannot see any difference in the two displayed lines of Figure 7-3:

- The `Console.WriteLine` method converts everything it gets into text. It does this silently using the `ToString` conversion behind the scenes.

- If you join some text with a number using the plus sign, the number gets automatically converted to text in C#. If you desire greater control, always write down `.ToString()` in connection with numbers.

# Formatting Numbers

In the previous exercise, you were busy with converting numbers into their textual representations. However, there are multiple ways that a single number can be expressed in a text form. You will now learn about decimal places, rounding, thousands separation, and so on.

## Task

In the present exercise, you will see several examples of the use of the `ToString` method to get nicely formatted numeric output (see Figure 7-4).

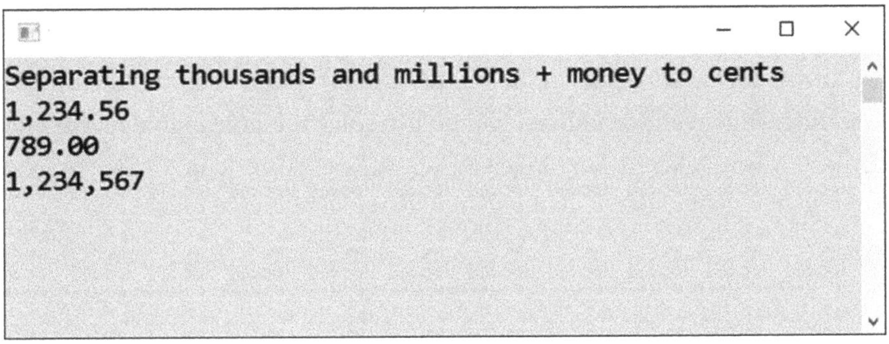

***Figure 7-4.*** *Nicely formatted output*

## Solution

Here is the code:

```
static void Main(string[] args)
{
    // Some money amounts and a number
    double amount = 1234.56;
    double anotherAmount = 789;
    int wholeNumber = 1234567;

    // Formatted outputs
    Console.WriteLine("Separating thousands and millions + money to cents");
    Console.WriteLine(amount.ToString("N2"));
    Console.WriteLine(anotherAmount.ToString("N2"));
    Console.WriteLine(wholeNumber.ToString("N0"));

    // Waiting for Enter
    Console.ReadLine();
}
```

Contrary to the earlier exercise, the ToString method call now has a parameter between parentheses. The *format string* specifies the way the output should look.

In the format strings used here, N means thousands separation is required, and two and zero denote the number of decimal places in the output.

## Localized Output

Ordinary number formatting (like in the previous task) works according to the Windows language setting. However, sometimes you do not want the output to depend on user settings. You may want a fixed-language setting, such as American, Czech, or whatever.

# Task

In this exercise, you will study the display of numbers in two different language styles, Czech and American (see Figure 7-5).

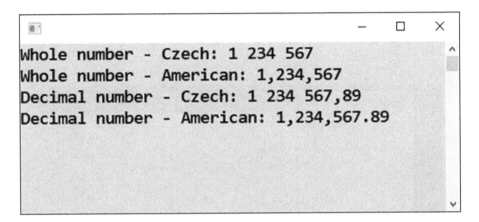

**Figure 7-5.**  *Two different number styles*

As you can see, in the Czech language, you use a space as the thousands separator and a comma as a decimal separator. The same comma is used as a thousands separator in American formatting, so you can imagine that letting a computer decide what language to use (according to Windows settings) can sometimes lead to a confusion and incorrect program behavior.

## Solution

First, add the appropriate using line at the top of the source code (with a reference to the System.Globalization namespace), as shown in Figure 7-6.

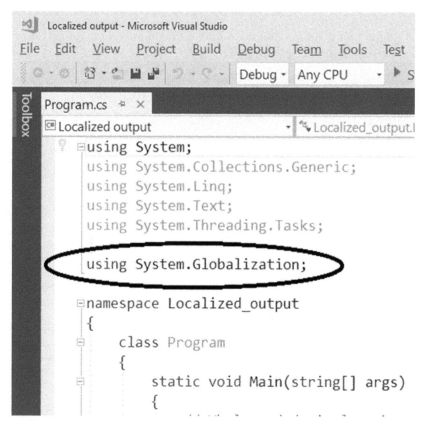

***Figure 7-6.***  *Adding a using line*

After that, enter the code into the Main method as usual:

```
static void Main(string[] args)
{
    // Whole and decimal number
    int wholeNumber = 1234567;
    double decimalNumber = 1234567.89;
```

```
// Localization objects
CultureInfo czech    = new CultureInfo("cs-CZ");
CultureInfo american = new CultureInfo("en-US");

// Localized output
Console.WriteLine("Whole number - Czech: "    + wholeNumber.
ToString("N0", czech));
Console.WriteLine("Whole number - American: " + wholeNumber.
ToString("N0", american));

Console.WriteLine("Decimal number - Czech: "    + decimalNumber.
ToString("N2", czech));
Console.WriteLine("Decimal number - American: " + decimalNumber.
ToString("N2", american));

// Waiting for Enter
Console.ReadLine();
}
```

# Concluding Notes

To finalize your knowledge of objects within the scope of this book, I will introduce you to some more object concepts. Please do not be worried if you do not understand them exactly right now. It is okay to just get an introduction to them at this stage of your study.

## Static Objects

First, I want to draw your attention toward the existence of two kinds of objects. There are "classic" objects such as DateTime, Random, and CultureInfo, and there are "static" objects such as Console, Environment, and Math.

You can have as many classic objects as you want in your program. For example, you had two DateTimes in the variables today and tomorrow. You also had three Randoms in the variables randomNumbers, randomNumbers1, and randomNumbers2.

Contrary to classic objects, static objects are always single—you have just one Console, just one Environment, and also just a single Math.

Also, you always create classic objects on demand, while the static ones exist since the program's start without any effort on your part.

Strictly using the official terminology, I should be talking about "classes with static components" rather than about "static objects." However, I prefer the latter, beginner-friendly term. It's better to be approximately beautiful than exactly ugly.

# Classes

Every documentation or textbook dealing with objects abounds with usage of the word *class*. So, what does this mean? To put it simply, a *class* is a synonym for an object data type. Instead of "an object of Random type," you can speak about "an object of the Random class." This means a class can also be viewed as the name of a certain type of objects.

# Relation Between Class and Object

From a different perspective, a class is also a C# source code defining what an object of a particular kind contains and how it behaves. You can also say that classes serve as templates for objects. For example, the Random class source code (which Microsoft has, not you) defines what properties and what methods *all* Randoms will have.

As a consequence, all Random objects behave in the same way because all of them are created from the same template, or from the same class. The same can be said about all DateTimes, all CultureInfos, and so on.

To put it another way, as a well-known maxim of object-oriented programming, an *object* is a class instance. The word *instance* means a single realization, or a single occurrence.

# Special Classes

You saw in this chapter that text, numbers, and so on, also behave like objects. Here are their corresponding classes:

| Data Type | Corresponding Class |
|-----------|---------------------|
| string | String |
| int | Int32 |
| double | Double |
| bool | Boolean |
| ... | ... |

In C#, you can use `string` and `String` interchangeably, `int` and `Int32` interchangeably, and so on. Of course, you need a `using System;` line at the top of your source code since all the corresponding classes belong to that particular namespace.

# Structures

In C#, you may encounter the term *structure* or *struct*, as well. What are structures?

Well, you can view them as something like lightweight classes. At a beginner's level, they are almost indistinguishable from normal classes, so you may simply substitute the word *class* wherever you see *structure* or *struct* for a long time.

For example, `DateTime` is the prime example of a structure. However, for the sake of simplicity, everywhere in this book I treat `DateTime` on equal terms with normal classes like `Random` or `CultureInfo`. The only subtle difference you might perceive when working at the level of this book is that `DateTime` objects do not necessarily have to be explicitly created, for example, via a constructor call. It is enough, though possibly not practical, to declare a variable of that type.

# Summary

In this chapter, you learned that even ordinary text and numbers can behave like objects. Specifically, you studied the following:

- `Length` property, plus `ToUpper` and `Contains` methods of text

- `ToString` method of numbers

In the latter case, you also saw that the output generated by the `ToString` method can be controlled by format strings (like N2, etc.) and language specifications (`CultureInfo` objects). In the future, you will find it convenient to use the `ToString` method with absolutely everything in C#, not just with numbers.

You got your first glimpse into object programming terminology. Specifically, note the following:

- Contrary to ordinary objects, static objects always exist in a single copy. While you can have as many `DateTimes` as you like, you always have precisely one `Console`.

- The word *class* is synonymous to "object data type." You will often read about objects of a specific class, which means "object of a particular type."

# PART II

# Calculations

# CHAPTER 8

# Input

Up to now, all of your programs have been manipulating data (numbers, text, and so on) that was either fixed directly in source code or drawn from the operating system (dates, random numbers, and so on). Typically, programs get their data from the user, which is what you will learn about in this chapter.

## Text Input

You will start your study of input with the simplest possible case.

## Task

You will write a program that accepts a single line of text from the user and immediately repeats the inputted text to the output (see Figure 8-1).

*Figure 8-1.* *The completed program*

© Radek Vystavěl 2017
R. Vystavěl, *C# Programming for Absolute Beginners*, https://doi.org/10.1007/978-1-4842-3318-4_8

## Solution

Here is the code:

```
static void Main(string[] args)
{
    // Reading single line of text (until user presses Enter key)
    string input = Console.ReadLine();

    // Outputting the input
    Console.WriteLine(input);

    // Waiting for Enter
    Console.ReadLine();
}
```

When you launch the program using the F5 key, you will see an empty screen. Enter a sentence and send it to the program using the Enter key.

## Better Input

In the previous program, the user may have no idea what to do. You have not told the user what to do. In this exercise, you will improve the input procedure.

## Task

You will modify the previous program in a way to give the user a hint about what she is supposed to do (see Figure 8-2).

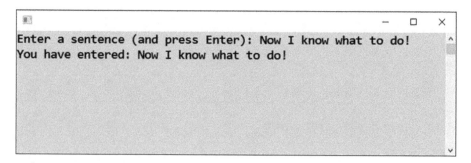

***Figure 8-2.*** *The improved program*

# Solution

Here is the code:

```
static void Main(string[] args)
{
    // Hinting user what we want from her
    Console.Write("Enter a sentence (and press Enter): ");

    // Reading line of text
    string input = Console.ReadLine();

    // Repeating to the output
    Console.WriteLine("You have entered: " + input);

    // Waiting for Enter
    Console.ReadLine();
}
```

# Discussion

Console.Write does not transfer the cursor to the next line, contrary to Console.WriteLine, which you have been using exclusively up to now.

# Numeric Input

In previous exercises, you were engaged with the input of text information from the user. Now you will switch to numbers, which are equally important.

# Task

You will write a program that takes a number from the user, stores it in a numeric variable, and finally repeats it to the user (see Figure 8-3).

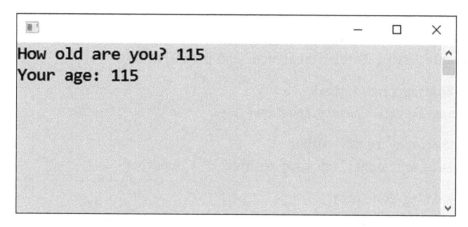

*Figure 8-3.* *Reading a number from the screen*

# Solution

Console.ReadLine always reads text even if its meaning is a number. If you want to hold a real number (i.e., a value of the int type), you have to manufacture it using the Convert.ToInt32 call.

```
static void Main(string[] args)
{
    // Prompting the user
    Console.Write("How old are you? ");

    // Reading line of text
    string input = Console.ReadLine();

    // CONVERTING TO NUMBER (of entered text)
    int enteredNumber = Convert.ToInt32(input);

    // Output of entered number
    Console.WriteLine("Your age: " + enteredNumber);

    // Waiting for Enter
    Console.ReadLine();
}
```

# Discussion

Strictly speaking, you have not actually needed a real number yet since you have not made any calculation on the numbers. However, this will change in next exercise. Here you were exploring numeric input in the simplest possible form.

# Calculation with Entered Number

You will now do your first calculation with the value entered by the user.

# Task

You will write a program that accepts a year of birth from the user and calculates her age afterward (see Figure 8-4).

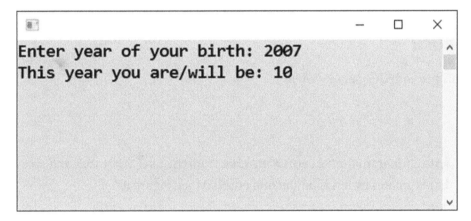

*Figure 8-4.  Calculating an age*

# Solution

Here is the solution:

```
static void Main(string[] args)
{
    // Prompting the user
    Console.Write("Enter year of your birth: ");

    // Reading line of text
    string input = Console.ReadLine();
```

```
    // CONVERING TO NUMBER (of entered text)
    int yearOfBirth = Convert.ToInt32(input);

    // Finding this year
    DateTime today = DateTime.Today;
    int thisYear = today.Year;

    // Calculating age
    int age = thisYear - yearOfBirth;

    // Outputting the result
    Console.WriteLine("This year you are/will be: " + age);

    // Waiting for Enter
    Console.ReadLine();
}
```

# Ten More

Let's continue with the calculations.

## Task

You will write a program that accepts a number from the user. After that, it displays a number that is greater by ten than the one entered (see Figure 8-5).

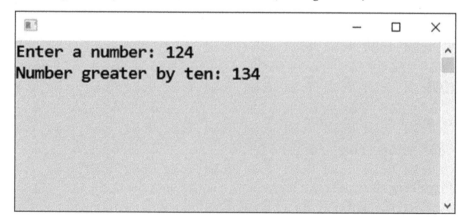

*Figure 8-5.* *Adding ten to a number*

# Solution

Here is the code:

```
static void Main(string[] args)
{
    // Number input
    Console.Write("Enter a number: ");
    string input = Console.ReadLine();
    int number = Convert.ToInt32(input);

    // Calculating
    int result = number + 10;

    // Displaying the result
    Console.WriteLine("Number greater by ten: " + result);

    // Waiting for Enter
    Console.ReadLine();
}
```

# Addition

You will take this step further now and make calculations with two numbers from the user.

# Task

You will write a program that sums two numbers entered by the user (see Figure 8-6).

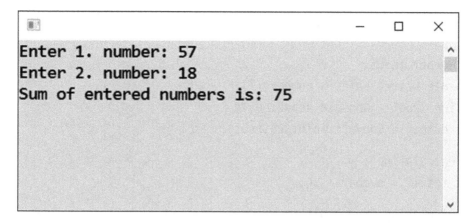

***Figure 8-6.*** *Summing two numbers*

# Solution

Here is the code:

```
static void Main(string[] args)
{
    // Input of 1. number
    Console.Write("Enter 1. number: ");
    string input1 = Console.ReadLine();
    int number1 = Convert.ToInt32(input1);

    // Input of 2. number
    Console.Write("Enter 2. number: ");
    string input2 = Console.ReadLine();
    int number2 = Convert.ToInt32(input2);

    // Calculating
    int result = number1 + number2;

    // Result output
    Console.WriteLine("Sum of entered numbers is: " + result);

    // Waiting for Enter
    Console.ReadLine();
}
```

# Incorrect Input

In the previous programs with numbers, if the user entered something other than a number, the program terminated with a *runtime error*. Production programs, however, should not behave like this. Now you will learn how to deal with a runtime error.

## Task

In this exercise, you will modify the previous program so that it correctly handles non-numeric input from the user (see Figure 8-7).

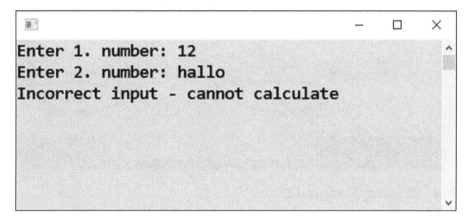

*Figure 8-7.* *Providing feedback for an error*

## Solution

Leave your last project opened, or open it again if you closed it already. In what follows, you will edit the project's `Program.cs` source code; specifically, you will insert a `try-catch` construct in an appropriate place.

Using your mouse, select the whole interior of `Main` excluding the last statement (`waiting for Enter`), exactly as shown in Figure 8-8. After that, right-click anywhere in the selected block and choose Snippet and then Surround With from context menu.

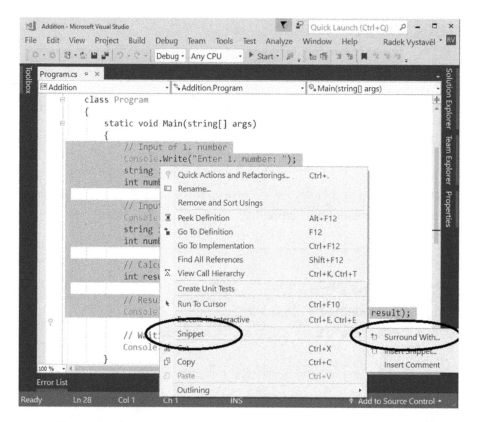

***Figure 8-8.*** *Choosing Surround With*

In the small pane that pops up, select Try (see Figure 8-9).

***Figure 8-9.*** *Selecting Try*

# What Happened

What happened? Visual Studio wrapped the selected lines into the `try` block, which consists of the word `try` and a pair of curly brackets. It also inserted a `catch` block, which includes the word `catch` and a pair of curly brackets, after the `try` block.

# Interior of the catch Part

Delete the statement `throw` inside the `catch` block and enter the following statement instead:

```
Console.WriteLine("Incorrect input - cannot calculate");
```

# Complete Solution

Here is the complete solution:

```
static void Main(string[] args)
{
    try
    {
        // Input of 1. number
        Console.Write("Enter 1. number: ");
        string input1 = Console.ReadLine();
        int number1 = Convert.ToInt32(input1);

        // Input of 2. number
        Console.Write("Enter 2. number: ");
        string input2 = Console.ReadLine();
        int number2 = Convert.ToInt32(input2);

        // Calculating
        int result = number1 + number2;

        // Result output
        Console.WriteLine("Sum of entered numbers is: " + result);
    }
    catch (Exception)
    {
```

```
        Console.WriteLine("Incorrect input - cannot calculate");
    }

    // Waiting for Enter
    Console.ReadLine();
}
```

## Testing

You can test your program both for numeric input and for nonsense now.

## Explanation

Statements in a try block are executed in a kind of "trial mode."

- When all of them succeed, execution in the try block proceeds normally, and the catch block is skipped afterward.

- When a statement fails, the rest of the try block is skipped, and statements in the catch block are executed instead.

## Summary

In this chapter, you entered a new level of programming skill. Up to now, you considered just the output from your program. Here you started dealing with the input from the user, first textual input and then numeric input.

Specifically, you learned the following:

- To get text input from the user using the Console.ReadLine method call.

- To display a hint to the user before requesting the input. For that purpose, you used the Console.Write method, which differs from its sister Console.WriteLine in that it does not terminate a line.

- To convert textual input of a number into its actual numeric representation using the Convert.ToInt32 method to make various calculations with it afterward.

In the final exercise, you considered the important situation of runtime errors, such as non-numeric inputs, for example. You learned to deal with them using the `try-catch` construct. The construct consists of two blocks.

- The `try` block surrounds statements executed "on trial." If everything goes OK, the `try` block does not change anything, and after its completion, the program's execution continues immediately after the whole `try-catch` construct.

- The `catch` block surrounds statements that are executed exclusively when an error appears during the `try` block processing. In the presence of the `catch` block, a statement in the `try` block that fails does not cause a runtime error and program termination. Instead, the error is "caught," and a specified alternative action is launched.

# CHAPTER 9

# Numbers

In previous chapter, you learned about input in general and numeric input in particular. You also did some simple calculations on numbers entered by the user. In this chapter, you will look at numbers in more detail. After all, a computer is called a computer because it computes frequently!

## Decimal Input

You will start with the task of reading a decimal number from the user.

## Task

You will write program that accepts a decimal number from the user and repeats it immediately on the screen (see Figure 9-1).

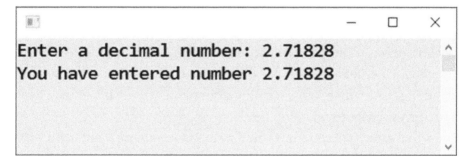

```
Enter a decimal number: 2.71828
You have entered number 2.71828
```

***Figure 9-1.*** *The final program*

109
© Radek Vystavěl 2017
R. Vystavěl, *C# Programming for Absolute Beginners*, https://doi.org/10.1007/978-1-4842-3318-4_9

## Solution

There are two differences between the input of whole and decimal numbers.

- You convert text input into a corresponding number by calling the Convert.ToDouble method.

- To store a converted number, you use a variable of type double.

Here is the code:

```
static void Main(string[] args)
{
    // Decimal input
    Console.Write("Enter a decimal number: ");
    string input = Console.ReadLine();
    double decimalNumber = Convert.ToDouble(input);

    // Repeating entered number to the output
    Console.WriteLine("You have entered number " + decimalNumber);

    // Waiting for Enter
    Console.ReadLine();
}
```

## Localized Numeric Input

In the previous exercise, the user enters a decimal separator according to the Windows language setting. This means a decimal point for the English language. However, it may mean something else in other languages. For example, a comma is used as a decimal separator in the Czech language.

In the current exercise, I will show you how to force numeric input in a specific localization, regardless of the Windows settings. You did a similar task concerning localized output earlier in the book; now you are going to concentrate on input.

# Task

The task is to write a program that reads a decimal number with two fixed-language settings, American and Czech.

# Solution

To work with specific localizations, use the `CultureInfo` object. Also, please do not forget to insert the `using System.Globalization;` line at the top of your source code.

Here is the code:

```
static void Main(string[] args)
{
    // AMERICAN
    CultureInfo american = new CultureInfo("en-US");
    try
    {
        // Input
        Console.Write("Enter American decimal number: ");
        string input = Console.ReadLine();
        double number = Convert.ToDouble(input, american);

        // Output
        Console.WriteLine("You have entered " + number);
    }
    catch (Exception)
    {
        // Error message
        Console.WriteLine("Incorrect input");
    }

    // CZECH
    CultureInfo czech = new CultureInfo("cs-CZ");
    try
    {
        // Input
        Console.WriteLine();
```

```
        Console.Write("Enter Czech decimal number: ");
        string input = Console.ReadLine();
        double number = Convert.ToDouble(input, czech);

        // Output
        Console.WriteLine("You have entered " + number);
    }
    catch (Exception)
    {
        // Error message
        Console.WriteLine("Incorrect input");
    }

    // Waiting for Enter
    Console.ReadLine();
}
```

# Testing and Conclusions

The following sections cover how this works.

## Test with a Decimal Point

Run your program and enter a number with a decimal point twice (see Figure 9-2).

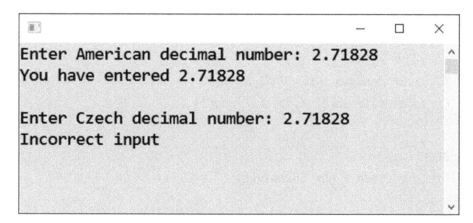

*Figure 9-2.* *Entering two numbers with decimal points*

The program accepts a point as a decimal separator when using the American localization. At the same time, it refuses a decimal point when using the Czech localization since a point is not a valid decimal separator in Czech.

## Test with a Decimal Comma

Run your program again and this time enter a number with decimal comma twice (see Figure 9-3).

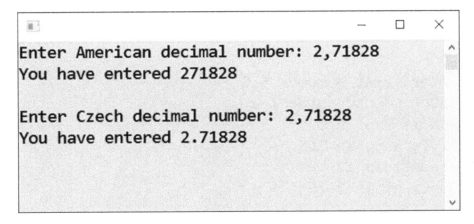

*Figure 9-3.* *Entering a number twice with a comma*

Now the program accepts the decimal comma as a valid separator in Czech.

When using the American localization, the program does not see any decimal number. It simply ignores the comma and converts the user input into a whole number!

## Further Conclusions

In this book, I am showing the output with decimal points in the figures. This is because I have not specified any localization in the output statements, and my Windows settings are currently set to American English. Both tests show that decimal input may betray you if you are not care enough. Just to remind you, if you enter a decimal number directly in your C# source code, you should always use a decimal point regardless of your settings.

# Basic Arithmetic

You are working with numbers in this chapter, so it is a good time to perform all four basic arithmetic operations.

## Task

You will write a program that accepts two decimal numbers from the user and displays the results of their addition, subtraction, multiplication, and division (see Figure 9-4).

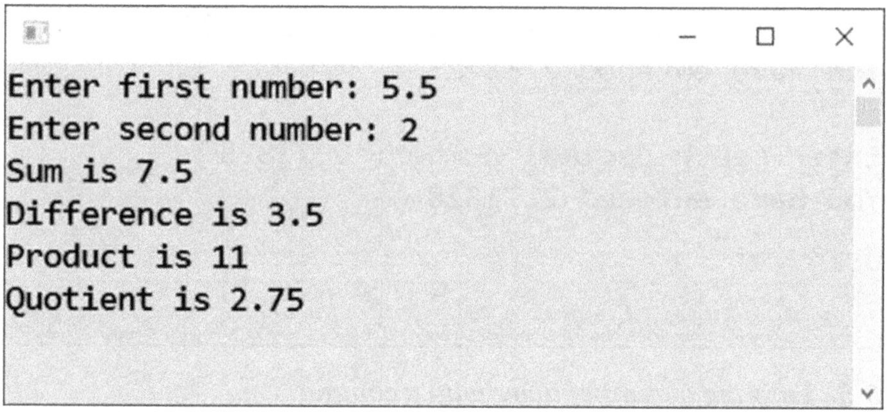

```
Enter first number: 5.5
Enter second number: 2
Sum is 7.5
Difference is 3.5
Product is 11
Quotient is 2.75
```

*Figure 9-4.* *Doing basic arithmetic*

## Solution

Here is the code:

```
static void Main(string[] args)
{
    // Inputs
    Console.Write("Enter first number: ");
    string input1 = Console.ReadLine();
    double number1 = Convert.ToDouble(input1);

    Console.Write("Enter second number: ");
    string input2 = Console.ReadLine();
    double number2 = Convert.ToDouble(input2);
```

```
// Calculations
double sum = number1 + number2;
double difference = number1 - number2;
double product = number1 * number2;
double quotient = number1 / number2;

// Output
Console.WriteLine("Sum is " + sum);
Console.WriteLine("Difference is " + difference);
Console.WriteLine("Product is " + product);
Console.WriteLine("Quotient is " + quotient);

// Waiting for Enter
Console.ReadLine();
}
```

# Mathematical Functions

When you do engineering or financial calculations, you often need more complex operations than the four basic ones shown in the previous exercise. Now you will see how to perform the complex operations using built-in (predefined) mathematical functions.

## Task

To get you a taste of the mathematical functions available, you will calculate the sine and the square root of the entered numbers in this task (see Figure 9-5).

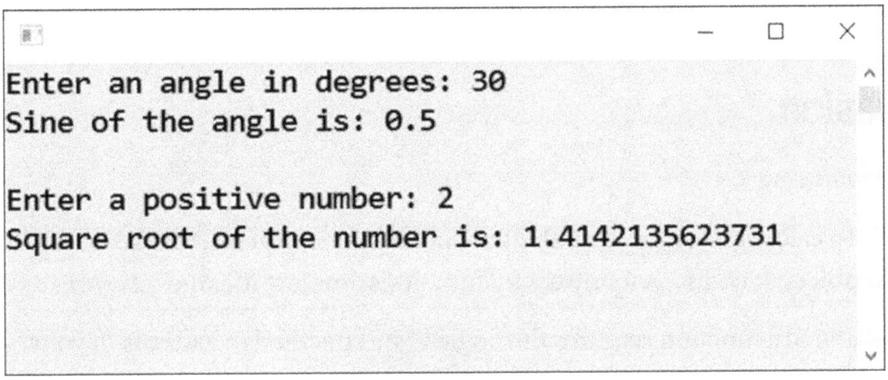

*Figure 9-5. Calculating the sine and the square root*

## Solution

Here is the code:

```
static void Main(string[] args)
{
    // Input of angle
    Console.Write("Enter an angle in degrees: ");
    string input = Console.ReadLine();
    double angleInDegrees = Convert.ToDouble(input);

    // Calculation and output of sine value
    double angleInRadians = angleInDegrees * Math.PI / 180;
    double result = Math.Sin(angleInRadians);
    Console.WriteLine("Sine of the angle is: " + result);

    // Input of a positive number
    Console.WriteLine();
    Console.Write("Enter a positive number: ");
    input = Console.ReadLine();
    double number = Convert.ToDouble(input);

    // Calculation and output of square root
    Console.WriteLine("Square root of the number is: " + Math.
    Sqrt(number));

    // Waiting for Enter
    Console.ReadLine();
}
```

## Discussion

Note the following:

- To calculate values of mathematical functions, you use the `Math` object; it contains many useful functions, not just the ones shown.

- The `Sin` function requires the angle to be specified in **radians**. If your input is in degrees, which is usually the case, you need to make a conversion.

- With the second input (a number), you "recycled" the variable `input` that was already used before; you used it a second time since you did not need the stored value anymore. However, this means you do not declare the variable a second time.

- You do not have to "recycle" variables; variables are not precious resources these days. But you can if you want, which is what I showed you.

- Contrary to the first calculation, you did not store the calculated square root into any variable. You directly wrote the calculation into the output statement (`WriteLine`).

- If the user enters a negative number, its square root cannot be calculated, and the result becomes `NaN` (which means "not-a-number").

# Integer Division

When programming, surprisingly often you will need to work with integer division, which is division with a remainder. For example, 33 divided by 7 is either 4.71428… normally or 4 with remainder 5.

On various computing platforms, you will do integer division differently from "normal" division. Unfortunately, in C#, you use the same operator, the slash (/), for both types. It works like this:

- If you put a slash between two values of the `int` type, the slash performs integer division.

- If at least one of the two values is of `double` type, the slash performs "normal" division.

This behavior may be the source of ugly, difficult-to-find errors. The behavior is 45 years old and stems from when the C language was created; unfortunately, several newer languages, such as C#, inherited the behavior. Just be aware of it and be careful when using a slash.

# Task

In this exercise, you will explore "normal" and integer divisions of the two numbers entered by the user (see Figure 9-6).

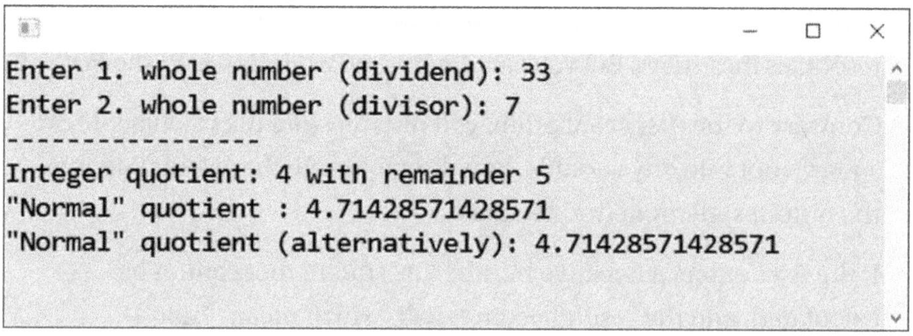

```
Enter 1. whole number (dividend): 33
Enter 2. whole number (divisor): 7
-----------------
Integer quotient: 4 with remainder 5
"Normal" quotient : 4.71428571428571
"Normal" quotient (alternatively): 4.71428571428571
```

**Figure 9-6.** *Exploring "normal" and integer divisions*

# Solution

Here is the code:

```
static void Main(string[] args)
{
    // Inputs
    Console.Write("Enter 1. whole number (dividend): ");
    string input1 = Console.ReadLine();
    int number1 = Convert.ToInt32(input1);

    Console.Write("Enter 2. whole number (divisor): ");
    string input2 = Console.ReadLine();
    int number2 = Convert.ToInt32(input2);

    // Integer calculations
    int integerQuotient = number1 / number2;
    int remainder = number1 % number2;

    // "Normal" calculations
    double number1double = number1;
    double number2double = number2;
    double normalQuotient = number1double / number2double;
```

```
    // Alternatively
    double normalQuotientAlternatively = (double)number1 / (double)number2;

    // Outputs
    Console.WriteLine("----------------");
    Console.WriteLine("Integer quotient: " + integerQuotient +
        " with remainder " + remainder);
    Console.WriteLine("\"Normal\" quotient : " + normalQuotient);
    Console.WriteLine("\"Normal\" quotient (alternatively): " +
    normalQuotientAlternatively);

    // Waiting for Enter
    Console.ReadLine();
}
```

## Discussion

Note the following:

- To compute the remainder, you use the % operator (percent sign).

- I have shown you two ways to force the entered values to doubles to achieve "normal" division.

  - Assignment to variables of type double.

  - *Type cast* to double; you prepend the value with the target type in parentheses.

## Summary

In this chapter, you explored numbers in a greater detail. You already knew about the difference between integers and decimal numbers in computing, and you knew how to read integers; in this chapter, you learned how to read decimals. You also found out that reading decimal numbers is language sensitive and can lead to surprising results when not being careful. If you do not specify the language to be used, the numbers are read using the Windows language settings. Specifically, you studied the following:

- Using the `Convert.ToDouble` method to convert textual user input into an actual decimal numbers

- Storing the converted value in a variable of type `double`

- Enforcing language settings with the `CultureInfo` object passed as a second parameter to the conversion method

In addition, you learned how to do basic arithmetic using the operators +, -, *, and /, and how to do more complex operations using built-in mathematical functions of the (static) `Math` object.

Finally, you explored integer division and its comparison to "normal" division and got to know about some tricky behavior of the slash operator, which performs the following:

- Integer division when used with two integers

- "Normal" division when at least one of the numbers is a decimal

You learned how to force "normal" division even with integers:

- Either assigning them to `double`-typed variables prior to calculation

- Typecasting them within the calculation

# CHAPTER 10

# Economic Calculations

In this chapter, you will learn how to count money. It's pretty simple, but you need to use some common sense.

## Currency Conversion

Performing simple economic calculations usually means doing currency conversions, which you will try in this section.

## Task

After accepting an amount in euros and the euro exchange rate, you will convert the amount to dollars (see Figure 10-1).

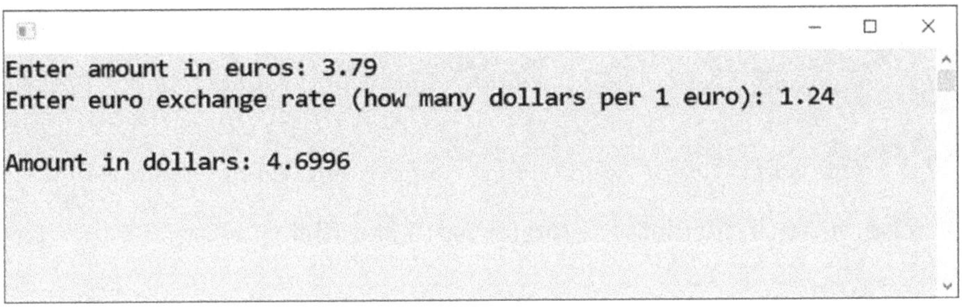

```
Enter amount in euros: 3.79
Enter euro exchange rate (how many dollars per 1 euro): 1.24

Amount in dollars: 4.6996
```

***Figure 10-1.*** *Converting to dollars*

© Radek Vystavěl 2017
R. Vystavěl, *C# Programming for Absolute Beginners*, https://doi.org/10.1007/978-1-4842-3318-4_10

## Solution

Here is the code:

```
static void Main(string[] args)
{
    // Inputs
    Console.Write("Enter amount in euros: ");
    string inputEuros = Console.ReadLine();
    double amountEuros = Convert.ToDouble(inputEuros);

    Console.Write("Enter euro exchange rate (how many dollars per 1 euro): ");
    string inputExchangeRate = Console.ReadLine();
    double euroEchangeRate = Convert.ToDouble(inputExchangeRate);

    // Calculation
    double amountDollars = amountEuros * euroEchangeRate;

    // Output
    Console.WriteLine();
    Console.WriteLine("Amount in dollars: " + amountDollars);

    // Waiting for Enter
    Console.ReadLine();
}
```

# Total Price

In this exercise, you will calculate the total price of an order.

## Task

Say one of your customers buys several items, some of them possibly multiple times. You need to calculate the total price including the shipping cost. In this program, the prices and amounts of two products, as well as the shipping price, will be fixed directly in the source code for simplicity (see Figure 10-2).

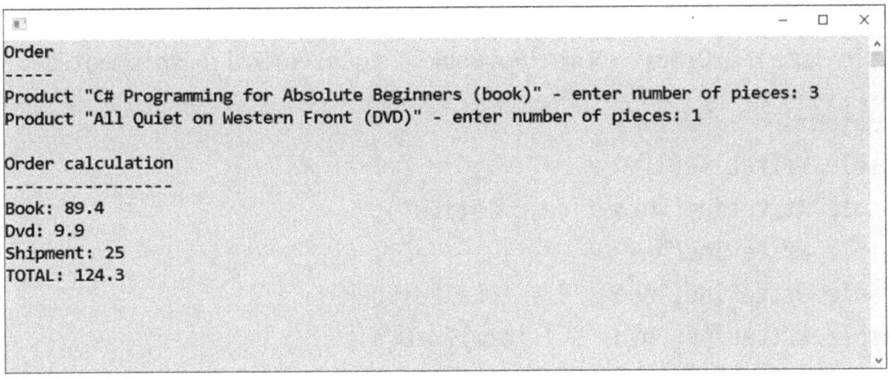

***Figure 10-2.*** *Calculating total costs*

# Solution

Here is the code:

```
static void Main(string[] args)
{
    // Fixed values
    const double bookPrice = 29.8;
    const double dvdPrice = 9.9;
    const double shipmentPrice = 25;

    // Inputs
    Console.WriteLine("Order");
    Console.WriteLine("-----");

    Console.Write("Product \"C# Programming for Absolute Beginners
    (book)\" - enter number of pieces: ");
    string inputBookPieces = Console.ReadLine();
    int bookPieces = Convert.ToInt32(inputBookPieces);

    Console.Write("Product \"All Quiet on Western Front (DVD)\" - enter
    number of pieces: ");
    string inputDvdPieces = Console.ReadLine();
    int dvdPieces = Convert.ToInt32(inputDvdPieces);

    // Calculations
    double totalForBook = bookPrice * bookPieces;
```

```
    double totalForDvd = dvdPrice * dvdPieces;
    double totalForOrder = totalForBook + totalForDvd + shipmentPrice;

    // Outputs
    Console.WriteLine();
    Console.WriteLine("Order calculation");
    Console.WriteLine("-----------------");
    Console.WriteLine("Book: " + totalForBook);
    Console.WriteLine("Dvd: " + totalForDvd);
    Console.WriteLine("Shipment: " + shipmentPrice);
    Console.WriteLine("TOTAL: " + totalForOrder);

    // Waiting for Enter
    Console.ReadLine();
}
```

## Discussion

Prepending fixed "variables" with const says they are *constants*, which are values that are not going to change in the course of the program run. Visual Studio does not allow you to assign new values to these "variables."

Personally, I do not use const often. I just wanted to show it to you in case you see it during the course of your work.

## Commissions

In capitalism, what matters most is not to create, produce, or plant something. The most important thing is to sell! And the person selling usually gets a commission, so you must learn how to calculate that.

## Task

You will write a program that accepts the price of a product and then calculates the percentage of commission for the merchant, distributor, and producer. From the data, it also calculates the income division among the three parties (see Figure 10-3).

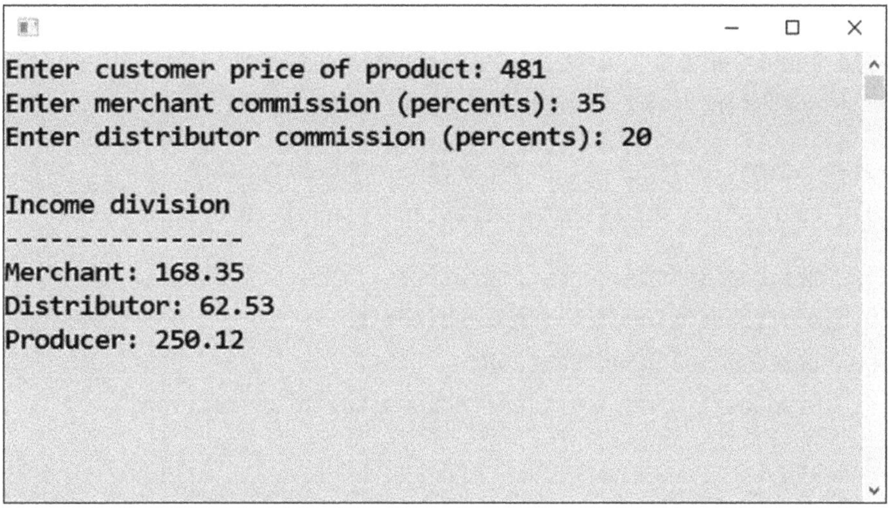

*Figure 10-3.* *Calculating commissions*

## Solution

Here is the code:

```
static void Main(string[] args)
{
    // Inputs
    Console.Write("Enter customer price of product: ");
    string inputPrice = Console.ReadLine();
    double customerPrice = Convert.ToDouble(inputPrice);

    Console.Write("Enter merchant commission (percents): ");
    string inputMerchantPercents = Console.ReadLine();
    int merchantPercents = Convert.ToInt32(inputMerchantPercents);

    Console.Write("Enter distributor commission (percents): ");
    string inputDistributorPercents = Console.ReadLine();
    int distributorPercents = Convert.ToInt32(inputDistributorPercents);
```

```
    // Calculations
    double coeficient1 = 1 - merchantPercents / 100.0;
    double coeficient2 = 1 - distributorPercents / 100.0;

    double wholesalePrice = customerPrice * coeficient1;
    double priceAfterCommissionSubtraction = wholesalePrice * coeficient2;

    double merchantIncome = customerPrice - wholesalePrice;
    double distributorIncome = wholesalePrice -
    priceAfterCommissionSubtraction;
    double producerIncome = priceAfterCommissionSubtraction;

    // Outputs
    Console.WriteLine();
    Console.WriteLine("Income division");
    Console.WriteLine("----------------");
    Console.WriteLine("Merchant: " + merchantIncome);
    Console.WriteLine("Distributor: " + distributorIncome);
    Console.WriteLine("Producer: " + producerIncome);

    // Waiting for Enter
    Console.ReadLine();
}
```

## Discussion

Sometimes commission percentages might be decimal numbers. I have chosen integers in this example because I wanted to show you how to correctly divide integers with a practical example. As you know, to perform "normal" division, you need at least one number—either in front of or after a slash—to be a double. That is why you use 100.0.

If you used 100 instead, the result would be surprising (see Figure 10-4).

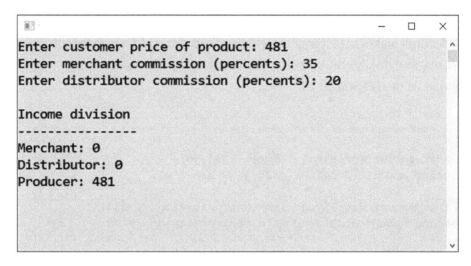

*Figure 10-4.* *Commission percents, incorrect*

Do you know why this happens? It's all because of rounding.

# Rounding

Money amounts are usually being rounded to cents. I will show you how to do this and what the difference is between rounding just for output and rounding for further calculations. The difference is small but sometimes significant. You might miss a cent and cause a problem for someone.

# Task

After the user enters two monetary amounts (possibly somehow calculated with more than two decimal places), the program will display them with percent precision, round them to cents, and finally compare the calculation with the original values to the one with rounded values (Figure 10-5).

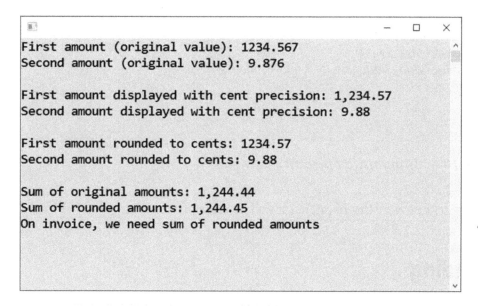

```
First amount (original value): 1234.567
Second amount (original value): 9.876

First amount displayed with cent precision: 1,234.57
Second amount displayed with cent precision: 9.88

First amount rounded to cents: 1234.57
Second amount rounded to cents: 9.88

Sum of original amounts: 1,244.44
Sum of rounded amounts: 1,244.45
On invoice, we need sum of rounded amounts
```

***Figure 10-5.***  *Rounding program*

# Solution

Here is the code:

```
static void Main(string[] args)
{
    // For simplicity, inputs are fixed in program
    // Some amounts, e.g. after commission calculations, cent fractions are
    possible
    double amount1 = 1234.567;
    double amount2 = 9.876;
```

```
// Displaying inputs (original values)
Console.WriteLine("First amount (original value): " + amount1);
Console.WriteLine("Second amount (original value): " + amount2);
Console.WriteLine();

// Rounding just for output
Console.WriteLine("First amount displayed with cent precision: " +
amount1.ToString("N2"));
Console.WriteLine("Second amount displayed with cent precision: " +
amount2.ToString("N2"));
Console.WriteLine();

// Rounding for further calculations + informative output
double roundedAmount1 = Math.Round(amount1, 2); // 2 = two decimal
places
double roundedAmount2 = Math.Round(amount2, 2);

Console.WriteLine("First amount rounded to cents: " + roundedAmount1);
Console.WriteLine("Second amount rounded to cents: " + roundedAmount2);
Console.WriteLine();

// Calculations
double sumOfOriginalAmounts = amount1 + amount2;
double sumOfRoundedAmounts = roundedAmount1 + roundedAmount2;

// Calculation outputs
Console.WriteLine("Sum of original amounts: " + sumOfOriginalAmounts.
ToString("N2"));
Console.WriteLine("Sum of rounded amounts: " + sumOfRoundedAmounts.
ToString("N2"));
Console.WriteLine("On invoice, we need sum of rounded amounts");

// Waiting for Enter
Console.ReadLine();
}
```

# Further Rounding

Sometimes rounding can be more complicated.

## Task

In this task, I will show you how to round to dollars, round to hundreds of dollars, always round down, and always round up (see Figure 10-6 and Figure 10-7).

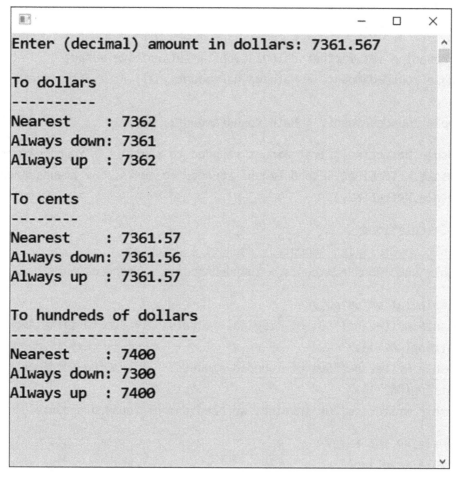

*Figure 10-6.* *More complicated rounding*

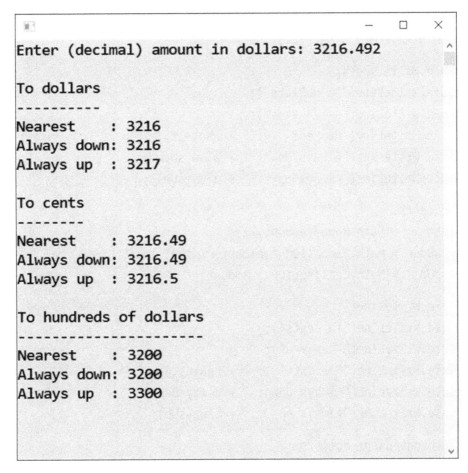

**Figure 10-7.** *Another number to round to dollars, cents, and hundreds of dollars*

## Solution

Here is the code:

```
static void Main(string[] args)
{
    // Input
    Console.Write("Enter (decimal) amount in dollars: ");
    string input = Console.ReadLine();
    double amount = Convert.ToDouble(input);

    // To dollars
    double nearest     = Math.Round(amount);
```

```
    double alwaysDown = Math.Floor(amount);
    double alwaysUp   = Math.Ceiling(amount);

    Console.WriteLine();
    Console.WriteLine("To dollars");
    Console.WriteLine("----------");
    Console.WriteLine("Nearest    : " + nearest);
    Console.WriteLine("Always down: " + alwaysDown);
    Console.WriteLine("Always up  : " + alwaysUp);

    // To cents
    nearest    = Math.Round(amount, 2);
    alwaysDown = Math.Floor(100 * amount) / 100;
    alwaysUp   = Math.Ceiling(100 * amount) / 100;

    Console.WriteLine();
    Console.WriteLine("To cents");
    Console.WriteLine("--------");
    Console.WriteLine("Nearest    : " + nearest);
    Console.WriteLine("Always down: " + alwaysDown);
    Console.WriteLine("Always up  : " + alwaysUp);

    // To hundreds of dollars
    nearest    = 100 * Math.Round(amount / 100);
    alwaysDown = 100 * Math.Floor(amount / 100);
    alwaysUp   = 100 * Math.Ceiling(amount / 100);

    Console.WriteLine();
    Console.WriteLine("To hundreds of dollars");
    Console.WriteLine("----------------------");
    Console.WriteLine("Nearest    : " + nearest);
    Console.WriteLine("Always down: " + alwaysDown);
    Console.WriteLine("Always up  : " + alwaysUp);

    // Waiting for Enter
    Console.ReadLine();
}
```

## Discussion

Of course, you can also display rounded values with cents, if you want, using - value. ToString("N2").

# Value-Added Tax

In Europe, we have a nice thing called value-added tax (VAT). Everybody is happy to pay more money for goods if it allows politicians to have a bigger budget for ... Actually, what for?

# Task

In this task, you will create a simple VAT calculator (see Figure 10-8). The program starts from the price a customer pays for a product and calculates the price without VAT (the merchant gets from the purchase) and also the VAT itself (what the merchant transfers to the tax administrator).

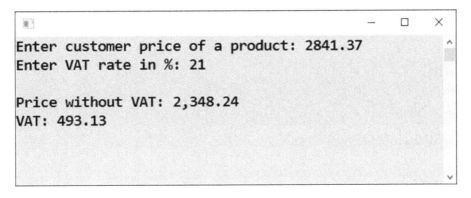

*Figure 10-8.* Calculating VAT

# Analysis

If you want to program something, you have to understand the essence of that something first. So, how does the European VAT work?

The foundation of the calculation is the price without VAT. To get this price, the appropriate percent part (for example, 21 percent) is added, and you get the price a customer pays. What is important is that the percents are calculated from the price without VAT, not from the customer price (see Figure 10-9)!

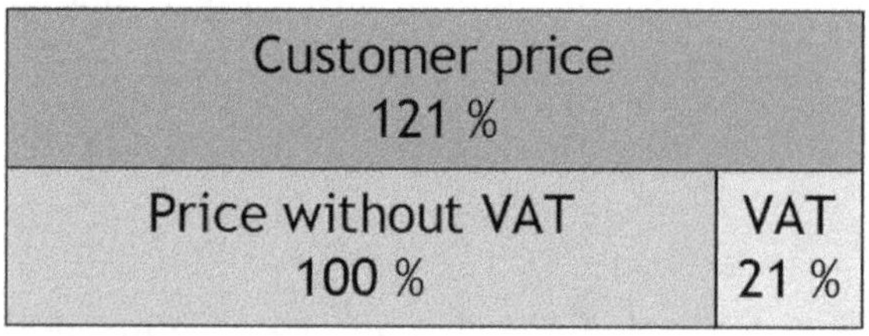

**Figure 10-9.**  *Understanding how the VAT works*

If the VAT rate is, for example, 21 percent, you need to divide the customer price by 1.21 to get the price without the VAT. For the general value of the tax rate, you calculate the divisor by adding the appropriate fraction to 1.

# Solution

Here is the code:

```
static void Main(string[] args)
{
    // Inputs
    Console.Write("Enter customer price of a product: ");
    string inputPrice = Console.ReadLine();
    double customerPrice = Convert.ToDouble(inputPrice);

    Console.Write("Enter VAT rate in %: ");
    string inputVatRate = Console.ReadLine();
    double vatRate = Convert.ToDouble(inputVatRate);

    // Calculations
    double divisor = 1 + vatRate / 100.0;
```

```
double calculatedPriceWithoutVat = customerPrice / divisor;
double priceWithoutVat = Math.Round(calculatedPriceWithoutVat, 2);
double vat = customerPrice - priceWithoutVat;

// Outputs
Console.WriteLine();
Console.WriteLine("Price without VAT: " + priceWithoutVat.
ToString("N2"));
Console.WriteLine("VAT: " + vat.ToString("N2"));

// Waiting for Enter
Console.ReadLine();
}
```

# Summary

In this chapter, you practiced calculations on a variety of real examples from the economic world. What is always the most important in calculations like these is to understand the real-world problem first. To understand how you would get the results without a program, start with a pencil, paper, and a calculator. It is also often helpful to structure your program appropriately, dividing the whole calculation into small pieces, and to use descriptive names for your variables.

Among other things, you learned how to do rounding. Specifically, you studied several built-in mathematical functions.

- You know how to use `Math.Round` for the most common rounding, in other words, to the nearest whole number. You can specify the number of required decimal places in the second parameter of the method call.

- You know how to use `Math.Floor` for always rounding down, in other words, to the greatest integer that is less than or equal to the number being rounded.

- You know how to use `Math.Ceiling` for always rounding up, in other words, to the lowest integer that is greater than or equal to the number being rounded.

You also learned a trick of how to round to hundreds, including dividing by 100 before rounding and multiplying by the same amount afterward.

# CHAPTER 11

# Calculations with Dates

In the previous chapter, you practiced calculations from the economic world. You will frequently need to do calculations with dates, too. Say you need to set the date when an invoice is due. Or say you want to calculate how many days an invoice is past due. Or, you might need to know the first and last days of a specific period like a month or a quarter. In this chapter, you'll learn how to do calculations with dates.

## Date Input

First, you will learn how to read a date from a user. I will show you some simple date arithmetic, too.

## Task

In this task, you will get a `DateTime` object based on the user input. After that, you will calculate the next and previous days (see Figure 11-1).

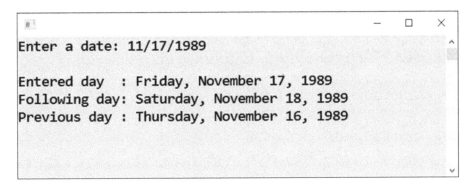

*Figure 11-1.* *Calculating the next and previous days*

© Radek Vystavěl 2017
R. Vystavěl, *C# Programming for Absolute Beginners*, https://doi.org/10.1007/978-1-4842-3318-4_11

# Solution

The point is to use the Convert.ToDateTime method. If the user enters a nonexistent day (February 29 of a nonleap year, for example), the method causes a runtime error that you can deal with using the try-catch construction.

```
static void Main(string[] args)
{
    try
    {
        // Text input of date
        Console.Write("Enter date: ");
        string input = Console.ReadLine();

        // Conversion to DateTime object
        DateTime enteredDate = Convert.ToDateTime(input);

        // Some calculations
        DateTime followingDay = enteredDate.AddDays(1);
        DateTime previousDay  = enteredDate.AddDays(-1);

        // Outputs
        Console.WriteLine();
        Console.WriteLine("Entered day  : " + enteredDate.
        ToLongDateString());
        Console.WriteLine("Following day: " + followingDay.
        ToLongDateString());
        Console.WriteLine("Previous day : " + previousDay.
        ToLongDateString());
    }
    catch (Exception)
    {
        // Treating incorrect input
        Console.WriteLine("Incorrect input");
    }

    // Waiting for Enter
    Console.ReadLine();
}
```

## Discussion

You can also call the Convert.ToDateTime method with two parameters instead of one. The second parameter is the language setting, which is the CultureInfo object you already know. This is similar to other conversion methods.

# Single Month

Now you will practice working with DateTime components and creating this object using a constructor call.

## Task

A user enters a date. This program displays the first and last days of the month in which the entered date falls (see Figure 11-2).

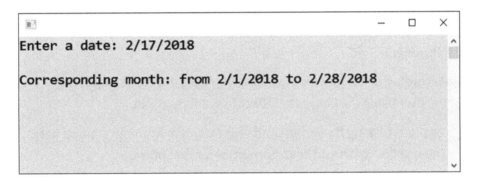

*Figure 11-2.* *Calcuating the first and last days of the month*

## Solution

Here is the code:

```
static void Main(string[] args)
{
    // Date input
    Console.Write("Enter a date: ");
    string input = Console.ReadLine();
    DateTime enteredDate = Convert.ToDateTime(input);
```

```
    // Calculations
    int enteredYear = enteredDate.Year;
    int enteredMonth = enteredDate.Month;

    DateTime firstDayOfMonth = new DateTime(enteredYear, enteredMonth, 1);
    DateTime lastDayOfMonth = firstDayOfMonth.AddMonths(1).AddDays(-1);

    // Outputs
    Console.WriteLine();
    Console.WriteLine("Corresponding month: " +
        "from " + firstDayOfMonth.ToShortDateString() +
        " to " + lastDayOfMonth.ToShortDateString());

    // Waiting for Enter
    Console.ReadLine();
}
```

## Discussion

Note the following:

- According to the previous exercise, you get a DateTime object from the user using the Convert.ToDateTime method call.

- You start picking the month and year numbers from the entered date. You use the Month and Year properties for that purpose.

- Using these numbers, you easily assemble the first day of the month because its day number is always 1.

- The last day of the month is not that easy because months differ in length. The trick is to add a month and subtract a day!

- Note that I do not store AddMonth's result anywhere. I directly call AddDays upon it instead. This is called *method chaining*.

- For the sake of simplicity, I do not deal with the possibility of incorrect input here.

# Quarter

Continuing with dates, I will show you some interesting tricks you must sometimes employ to get the correct results.

## Task

For the entered day, this program will display the beginning, end, and number (from 1 to 4) of the year's quarter that the day belongs to (see Figure 11-3 and Figure 11-4).

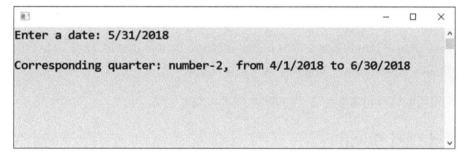

*Figure 11-3.*  *Showing the corresponding quarter*

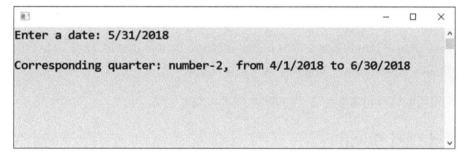

*Figure 11-4.*  *Showing the corresponding quarter, another example*

## Analysis

The key to this task is to determine the quarter's number. From that, the quarter's first month follows.

## Quarter's Number

You need to transform the month number into the quarter's number like this:

- Month 1, 2, or 3 = 1
- Month 4, 5, or 6 = 2
- Month 7, 8, or 9 = 3
- Month 10, 11, or 12 = 4

This is a beautiful case of integer division use. You can see that you need to add 2 to the month number first and perform integer division by 3 after that.

```
int numberOfQuarter = (enteredMonth + 2) / 3;
```

## Quarter's First Month Number

If you already have the quarter's number, you get the quarter's first month like this:

- 1 (January) for the first quarter
- 4 (April) for the second quarter
- 7 (July) for the third quarter
- 10 (October) for the fourth quarter

You may realize that the quarter's number has to be multiplied by 3. To get the correct results, you need to subtract 2 subsequently.

```
int monthOfQuarterStart = 3 * numberOfQuarter - 2;
```

## First and Last Days

Having the first month available, you can proceed in steps similar to the previous exercise. To get the first day, you use the DateTime constructor with the day number set to 1. To get the last day, you add three months and subtract one day.

# Solution

Here is the code:

```
static void Main(string[] args)
{
    // Date input
    Console.Write("Enter a date: ");
    string input = Console.ReadLine();
    DateTime enteredDate = Convert.ToDateTime(input);

    // Calculations
    int enteredYear = enteredDate.Year;
    int enteredMonth = enteredDate.Month;

    int numberOfQuarter = (enteredMonth + 2) / 3;
    int monthOfQuarterStart = 3 * numberOfQuarter - 2;
    DateTime firstDayOfQuarter = new DateTime(enteredYear,
    monthOfQuarterStart, 1);
    DateTime lastDayOfQuarter = firstDayOfQuarter.AddMonths(3).AddDays(-1);

    // Outputs
    Console.WriteLine();
    Console.WriteLine("Corresponding quarter: " +
        "number-" + numberOfQuarter +
        ", from " + firstDayOfQuarter.ToShortDateString() +
        " to " + lastDayOfQuarter.ToShortDateString());

    // Waiting for Enter
    Console.ReadLine();
}
```

# Date Difference

You frequently need to calculate the time span between two specific dates, in other words, how many days or years have passed between the entered dates. This is what you will study now.

# Task

A user enters the date of her birth. The program displays how many days the world is happy to have her (see Figure 11-5).

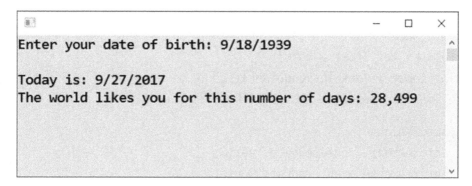

***Figure 11-5.*** *Calculating how many days alive*

# Solution

As you can see, you need to subtract the birth date from today's date. When you subtract dates, the result is a TimeSpan object. With this object in hand, you can use one of its many properties. You will use the Days property in this exercise.

Here is the code:

```
static void Main(string[] args)
{
    // Input
    Console.Write("Enter your date of birth: ");
    string input = Console.ReadLine();
    DateTime dateOfBirth = Convert.ToDateTime(input);

    // Today
    DateTime today = DateTime.Today;

    // Date difference
    TimeSpan difference = today - dateOfBirth;
    int numberOfDays = difference.Days;

    // Output
    Console.WriteLine();
```

```
    Console.WriteLine("Today is: " + today.ToShortDateString());
    Console.WriteLine("The world likes you for this number of days: " +
    numberOfDays.ToString("N0"));

    // Waiting for Enter
    Console.ReadLine();
}
```

# Time Zones and UTC

If you want to store the moment when something happened (e.g., to log orders, issues, and so on), you may be unpleasantly surprised by daylight saving time. Or, maybe more important, say you are creating a program that will operate across the globe. You will have to work with different time zones.

To handle these cases, it is good to know how to work with Universal Time Coordinated (UTC), which is the time at the zeroth meridian free from food additives. Pardon me, I mean free from daylight saving. UTC is simply time-zone independent.

It is also good to get acquainted with DateTimeOffset objects that contain time zone information in addition to the date and time.

## Task

In this exercise, I will show you how to work both with UTC and with the time zones included in a DateTimeOffset object. You will make a program that works with the current time (see Figure 11-6).

```
Now: 9/27/2017 1:11:15 PM
UTC now: 9/27/2017 11:11:15 AM
Now (including time zone): 9/27/2017 1:11:15 PM +02:00
Time zone (offset against UTC): 2
UTC now (including time zone): 9/27/2017 11:11:15 AM +00:00
```

***Figure 11-6.*** *DateTimeOffset object*

## Solution

Here is the code:

```
static void Main(string[] args)
{
    // Current time serves as input
    DateTime now = DateTime.Now;
    DateTime utcNow = DateTime.UtcNow;
    DateTimeOffset completeInstant = DateTimeOffset.Now;
    DateTimeOffset utcCompleteInstant = DateTimeOffset.UtcNow;

    // Outputs
    Console.WriteLine("Now: " + now);
    Console.WriteLine("UTC now: " + utcNow);
    Console.WriteLine("Now (including time zone): " + completeInstant);
    Console.WriteLine("Time zone (offset against UTC): " + completeInstant.
    Offset.TotalHours);
    Console.WriteLine("UTC now (including time zone): " +
    utcCompleteInstant);

    // Waiting for Enter
    Console.ReadLine();
}
```

Please note that some variables are of the DateTime type, while others are of the DateTimeOffset type.

## Summary

In this chapter, you quite thoroughly learned how to do calculations with dates.

You started by getting a date from the user using the Convert.ToDateTime method and followed with getting a date from the specified year, month, and day using DateTime's constructor call (new DateTime...).

In your calculations, you made appropriate use of various properties of DateTime objects, such as Day, Month, or Year, as well as its methods, such as AddDays, for example. Also, to calculate a quarter's number, you used integer division to your advantage.

Further, you got acquainted with how to calculate the difference between any two given dates and what to do with the result. Specifically, you used the `TimeSpan` object.

Finally, we discussed UTC and time zones to facilitate programs operating across multiple zones and to handle leaps of time due to daylight saving correctly. Specifically, you learned about the `DateTimeOffset` object.

# CHAPTER 12

# Understanding Different Kinds of Numbers

In this chapter, you will study several more advanced topics concerning numbers and calculations, such as more numeric types, memory consumption, and overflow. If you do not need this much detail at this time, you can safely skip this chapter or just skim it.

## More Numeric Types

You already know that there is a distinction between whole numbers and decimal numbers in computing. You use the `int` type for whole numbers, and you use the `double` type for decimal numbers.

But there are other numeric data types in C#. Although many of them exist mainly for historical reasons and you will probably never use them, it is good to know about them at least.

© Radek Vystavěl 2017
R. Vystavěl, *C# Programming for Absolute Beginners*, https://doi.org/10.1007/978-1-4842-3318-4_12

# Task

You will write a program that displays an overview of all the C# numeric data types. For each type, its range of possible values will be printed (see Figure 12-1).

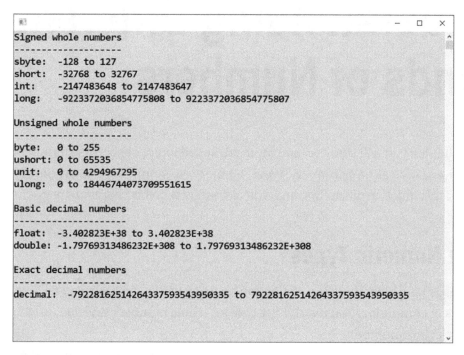

***Figure 12-1.*** *Printing all numeric data types*

# Solution

Here is the code:

```
static void Main(string[] args)
{
    // Immediately outputs
    Console.WriteLine("Signed whole numbers");
    Console.WriteLine("--------------------");
    Console.WriteLine("sbyte:  " + sbyte.MinValue + " to " +
    sbyte.MaxValue);
    Console.WriteLine("short:  " + short.MinValue + " to " +
    short.MaxValue);
```

```
Console.WriteLine("int:    " + int.MinValue + " to " + int.MaxValue);
Console.WriteLine("long:   " + long.MinValue + " to " + long.MaxValue);
Console.WriteLine();

Console.WriteLine("Unsigned whole numbers");
Console.WriteLine("---------------------");
Console.WriteLine("byte:   " + byte.MinValue + " to " + byte.MaxValue);
Console.WriteLine("ushort: " + ushort.MinValue + " to " + ushort.
MaxValue);
Console.WriteLine("unit:   " + uint.MinValue + " to " + uint.MaxValue);
Console.WriteLine("ulong:  " + ulong.MinValue + " to " + ulong.
MaxValue);
Console.WriteLine();

Console.WriteLine("Basic decimal numbers");
Console.WriteLine("---------------------");
Console.WriteLine("float:  " + float.MinValue + " to " + float.MaxValue);
Console.WriteLine("double: " + double.MinValue + " to " + double.
MaxValue);
Console.WriteLine();

Console.WriteLine("Exact decimal numbers");
Console.WriteLine("---------------------");
Console.WriteLine("decimal:  " + decimal.MinValue + " to " + decimal.
MaxValue);

// Waiting for Enter
Console.ReadLine();
}
```

## Note

To display the ranges, I have used the `MinValue` and `MaxValue` properties of all the numeric data types.

# Discussion

The following sections discuss this program.

## Unsigned Numbers

The results printed by the program show that some data types do not allow the storage of negative numbers! However, these *unsigned numbers* are rarely used, with the exception of the `byte` type, which you use when reading binary data from a file, a database, or a web service.

Contrary to their signed counterparts, unsigned numbers usually begin with a *u*, meaning "unsigned." Similarly, the signed type `sbyte` starts with an *s*, meaning the "signed" variant of the much more important `byte`.

## Decimal Numbers

Decimal type ranges are displayed in scientific notation (also called *exponential notation*). For example, the greatest `float` number is displayed as 3.4E+38, which means 3.4 times 10 to the 38th power. This is a really big number, isn't it?

Decimal types differ also in their precision. While the `float` type stores a decimal value with approximately 7 significant digits, the `double` type offers a precision of about 15 significant digits, and the `decimal` type offers 28 digits.

## Special Type decimal

The decimal data type is somewhat special. Because of the following reasons, it is preferably used when working with currency:

- It stores cent values exactly. For example, the amount of 12.80 will be stored precisely as 12.80 rather than something like 12.7999999999, which might happen using other types.

- Because of a large number of significant digits, the decimal data type allows you to represent large amounts of money and still keep the cent precision.

However, both of these reasons are not as convincing as they might seem. If you perform rounding correctly, you can store cents exactly with the double type. And frankly speaking, you usually need to solve other problems than that of whether double 15 digits are enough for money!

Moreover, many things are easier with the double type, which is why I use preferably double for decimals in this book.

One last note: calculations with the decimal type are *much* slower (in fact, hundreds of times slower) than the same calculations with the double type. This does not matter if you crunch just a few numbers, but the difference can be significant in large data sets.

# Memory Consumption

If you know something about bits and bytes, it may have occurred to you that the type ranges differ because of the memory space that is available to the corresponding types. This is exactly right, and you will learn more about it in this section.

# Task

In this section, you will write a program that tells you how many bytes of memory each type uses (see Figure 12-2).

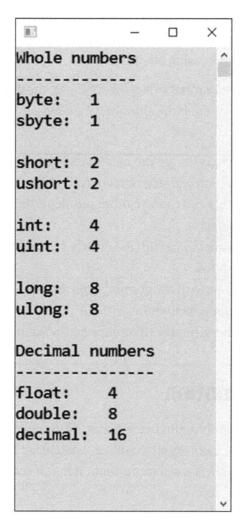

*Figure 12-2. Displaying the number of bytes each type uses*

# Solution

Here is the code:

```
static void Main(string[] args)
{
    // Outputs
    Console.WriteLine("Whole numbers");
    Console.WriteLine("-------------");
    Console.WriteLine("byte:  " + sizeof(byte));
    Console.WriteLine("sbyte:  " + sizeof(sbyte));
    Console.WriteLine();
    Console.WriteLine("short:  " + sizeof(short));
    Console.WriteLine("ushort: " + sizeof(ushort));
    Console.WriteLine();
    Console.WriteLine("int:    " + sizeof(int));
    Console.WriteLine("uint:   " + sizeof(uint));
    Console.WriteLine();
    Console.WriteLine("long:   " + sizeof(long));
    Console.WriteLine("ulong:  " + sizeof(ulong));
    Console.WriteLine();
    Console.WriteLine("Decimal numbers");
    Console.WriteLine("---------------");
    Console.WriteLine("float:   " + sizeof(float));
    Console.WriteLine("double:  " + sizeof(double));
    Console.WriteLine("decimal: " + sizeof(decimal));
    Console.WriteLine();

    // Waiting for Enter
    Console.ReadLine();
}
```

# Connections

It is possible to connect the results of the current and previous programs. For example, let's discuss the important int type. It uses 4 bytes, or 32 bits of memory. This means 2 to the 32nd power of possible values, which is more than 4 billion. int is a signed type, so you have 2 billion for positive numbers and 2 billion for negative numbers. Its unsigned counterpart uint has all 4 billion values for positive numbers (and, of course, zero).

# Discussion

You may feel confused about the variety of numeric data types. To help you understand them, here is a summary of when you should use each one:

- int: For regular work with values that are intrinsically integers (for example, counts of something).

- double: For regular work with values that may be decimal (for example, measured values) or values you do math with. Money amounts are also mostly OK.

- byte: For work with binary data.

- long: For big integer values such as file sizes, payment identifications (for example, ten digits may be required), or multiplication results of regular (whole) values.

- decimal: A common choice for money amounts.

The other types are not used that often.

# Overflow

When program calculates a value that does not "fit" into an appropriate type's range, what happens is called *overflow*. The behavior of your program can be very strange, as shown in Figure 12-3.

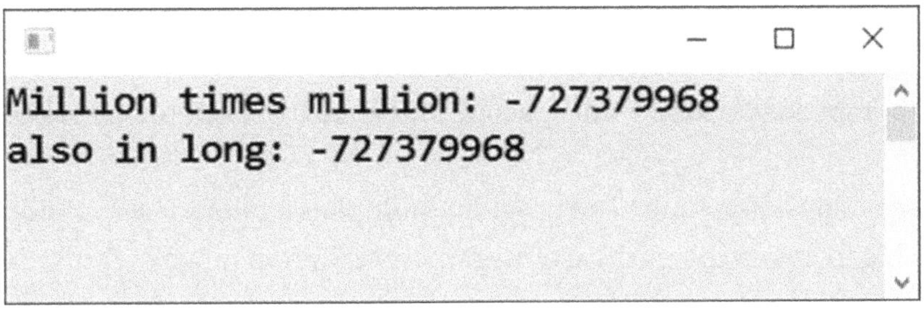

**Figure 12-3.** *Overflow*

Overflow can occur especially when multiplying because multiplying results in large numbers.

# Task

In this section, you will write a program that tries to calculate a million times a million.

# Solution

Here is the code:

```
static void Main(string[] args)
{
    // Multiplying million by million
    int million = 1000000;
    int result = million * million;
    long resultInLong = million * million;

    // Outputs
    Console.WriteLine("Million times million: " + result);
    Console.WriteLine("also in long: " + resultInLong);

    // Waiting for Enter
    Console.ReadLine();
}
```

## Discussion

What the program does is totally unexpected. You need to be aware of this kind of anomaly.

What is actually happening? The program multiplies a million by a million. The result is too big to fit into the positive or negative two-billion range of the 32-bit signed int type. So, the computer simply throws away the upper bits, resulting in complete nonsense.

Please note that you get the same nonsense even when you store the result in a long-typed variable. That nonsense, which throws away the bits greater than 32, arises during calculation. According to C# rules, int times int is simply int regardless of where you store the result.

## Dealing with Overflow

The previous program displayed an incorrect result. Now you will see what can be done about it.

## Task

Here are two possibilities of how to handle overflow problems:

- If you do not expect a big value and it appears anyway, the program should at least crash or let you know about the problem. Displaying a nonsense value is the worst alternative. Users trust their computers and can make wrong decisions based upon believing incorrect results.

- If you have an idea that int might be insufficient, you can make the calculation correctly with the following solution.

# Solution

The new project source code follows:

```
static void Main(string[] args)
{
    // 0. Preparation
    int million = 1000000;

    // 1. Crash at least, we do not
    //     definitely want a nonsense
    Console.WriteLine("1. calculation");
    try
    {
        long result = million * million;
        Console.WriteLine("Million times million:" + result);
    }
    catch (Exception)
    {
        Console.WriteLine("I cannot calculate this.");
    }

    // 2. Correct calculation of a big value
    Console.WriteLine("2. calculation");
    long millionInLong = million;
    long correctResult = millionInLong * millionInLong;
    Console.WriteLine("Million times million: " + correctResult.
    ToString("N0"));

    // 3. Alternative calculation of a big valule
    Console.WriteLine("3. calculation");
    long correctResultAlternatively = (long)million * (long)million;
    Console.WriteLine("Million times million: " +
    correctResultAlternatively.ToString("N0"));

    // Waiting for Enter
    Console.ReadLine();
}
```

## Note

However, this code does not solve everything. When you immediately launch the program, the first calculation is still going to be wrong. People sometimes take `try-catch` as a kind of panacea, but it is definitely not. You need something else, as discussed next.

## Settings in Visual Studio

You need to set up your project in Visual Studio so that it reports overflow out of the program instead of sweeping it under the rug.

From the Visual Studio menu, choose Project and then <Project name> Properties (see Figure 12-4).

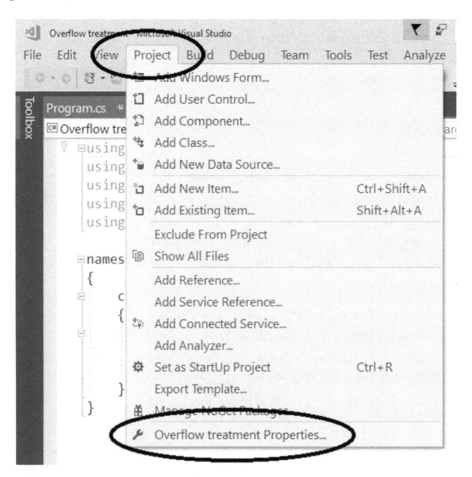

***Figure 12-4.*** *Opening the properties*

Choose the Build tab next, scroll vertically (and maybe also horizontally) so that you can see the Advanced button (it is really hidden!), and then click that button (see Figure 12-5).

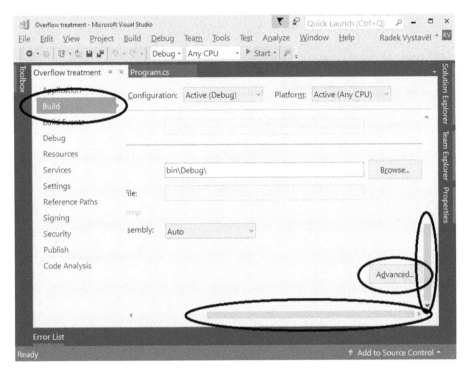

***Figure 12-5.***  *Build tab*

In the dialog that appears, select the "Check for arithmetic overflow/underflow" check box and confirm by clicking the OK button (see Figure 12-6).

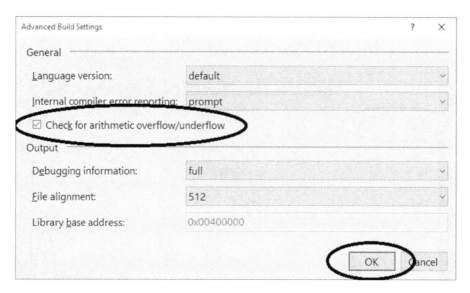

***Figure 12-6.*** *"Check for arithmetic overflow/underflow" check box*

Your project is finally ready to run now.

# Results

Now the program behaves according to expectations, as shown in Figure 12-7.

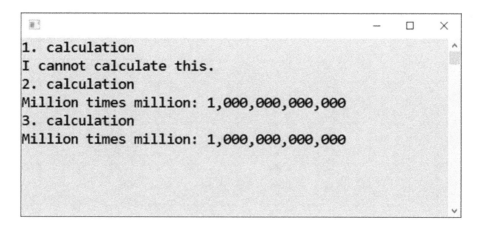

***Figure 12-7.*** *Multiplying a million by a million*

## First Alternative

The first calculation correctly reports a problem. Omitting `try-catch` would cause a runtime error, but at least it does not display an incorrect result.

## Other Alternatives

A correct calculation converts the million into a `long` type *before* the calculation starts. Here are two ways to perform this conversion:

- Assigning the million to a variable of type `long`

- Using an explicit *type cast* with `(long)million`

If you do not require precise integer arithmetic, you might also calculate in the `double` type. Unless you solve some very exotic math, `double` does not have a chance to overflow.

# Summary

In this chapter, you studied advanced number calculations. You got to know all the numeric data types that are available in C#. The types differ in whether they allow integers or decimals, and they differ also in the ranges of allowed values. Types for decimals mutually differ also in the precision with which the number is stored.

At the beginner level, knowledge of `int` and `double` is enough; you can always work using them only. When you become more experienced, you might also use the following:

- The `long` type for big integers such as file sizes, ten-digit payment numbers, or multiplication results of moderately sized numbers

- The `decimal` type for working with currency

- The `byte` type for working with binary data

You also studied the question of overflow. When a calculated value is too big to fit into the range of a particular data type, nonsense results. The default behavior of Visual Studio is to continue as normally. However, now you know how to change the settings to cause a runtime error at least, because continuing with the incorrect result is the worst alternative.

The best alternative is to avoid the overflow completely by choosing a data type with an appropriate range. However, keep in mind that changing the type of variable used to store the result may not be enough. For example, `int` multiplied by `int` is always `int` with a maximum value of about 2 billion, regardless of where you store it. It may be suitable to convert the number into a `long` type before the calculation.

# CHAPTER 13

# Accumulating Values

Up to now, you have worked with variables where you stored a value that you later used. After the initial assignment, the value of the variable did not change. Now you are ready to go to the next step, which is to study a case when a variable's value changes during the program run, in other words, when a new value is determined from the old one.

## Ten More, Revisited

First you will return to the task of adding ten to a number, which you studied in Chapter 8. The program's goal is to present a value that is greater by ten than the number entered by the user (see Figure 13-1).

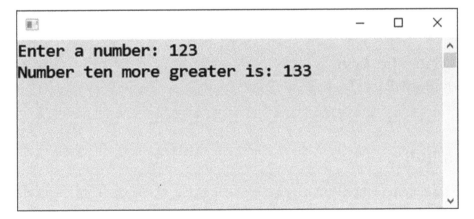

*Figure 13-1.* *Displaying the user's number plus ten*

© Radek Vystavěl 2017
R. Vystavěl, *C# Programming for Absolute Beginners*, https://doi.org/10.1007/978-1-4842-3318-4_13

# Task

You will now solve this task in a new way; specifically, you will store the calculation result in the same variable where you originally stored the entered number.

This is not necessarily a better solution, but you will learn how to build upon it further in later sections.

# Solution

Here is the code:

```
static void Main(string[] args)
{
    // Input
    Console.Write("Enter a number: ");
    string input = Console.ReadLine();
    int number = Convert.ToInt32(input);

    // Calculation
    number = number + 10;

    // Result output
    Console.WriteLine("Number ten more greater is: " + number);

    // Waiting for Enter
    Console.ReadLine();
}
```

# Discussion

The core statement of the solution is as follows: number = number + 10;. This statement is unusual in the sense that the same thing—the variable number—appears on both sides of the equal sign!

The computer executes the statement like this: "Take the present value of the variable number, add ten to it, and store the result as the new value of the variable number." Thus, the net result of the statement is augmenting number's value by ten.

# Compound Assignment

There is a nice shortcut for doing the same thing, which is called *compound assignment*. You will study this now.

## Task

You will solve the previous exercise using the more concise compound assignment.

## Solution

Here is the code:

```
static void Main(string[] args)
{
    // Input
    Console.Write("Enter a number: ");
    string input = Console.ReadLine();
    int number = Convert.ToInt32(input);

    // Calculation using compound assignment
    number += 10; // same as number = number + 10;

    // Result output
    Console.WriteLine("Number ten more greater is: " + number);

    // Waiting for Enter
    Console.ReadLine();
}
```

## Note

In this code, you use the compound assignment operator (+=), which is a shortcut that does the same thing as the previous solution. You will see compound assignments in all C-family programming languages.

# Further Compound Assignments

Did you like compound assignment? There are even more similar assignments to use when working with other arithmetic operations.

## Task

I will show you a program that illustrates compound assignment in connection with subtraction, multiplication, and division (see Figure 13-2).

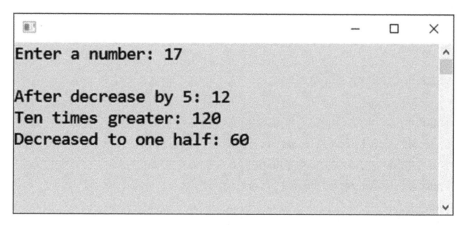

*Figure 13-2.*  *Compound assignment*

## Solution

Here is the code:

```
static void Main(string[] args)
{
    // Input
    Console.Write("Enter a number: ");
    string input = Console.ReadLine();
    int number = Convert.ToInt32(input);
    Console.WriteLine();

    // With subtraction
    number -= 5; // same as number = number - 5;
    Console.WriteLine("After decrease by 5: " + number);
```

```
    // With multiplication
    number *= 10; // same as number = number * 10;
    Console.WriteLine("Ten times greater: " + number);

    // With division
    number /= 2; // same as number = number / 2;
    Console.WriteLine("Decreased to one half: " + number);

    // Waiting for Enter
    Console.ReadLine();
}
```

## Note

The program works with the same variable every time!

The division here is integer division since both number and 2 are ints.

# Incrementing and Decrementing

By far the most frequent change for a variable is a change by 1. That is why there are special super-concise ways for how to make such calculations.

## Task

You'll now get acquainted with the increment operator (++) and the decrement operator (--), as shown in Figure 13-3.

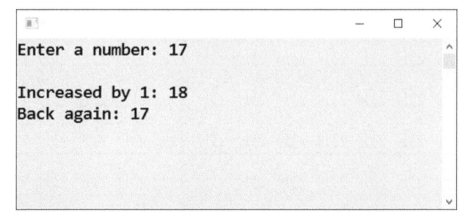

***Figure 13-3.*** *Increment and decrement operators*

## Solution

Here is the code:

```
static void Main(string[] args)
{
    // Input
    Console.Write("Enter a number: ");
    string input = Console.ReadLine();
    int number = Convert.ToInt32(input);

    // Increasing by 1 using INCREMENT OPERATOR
    number++; // same as number = number + 1;
    Console.WriteLine("Increased by 1: " + number);

    // Decreasing by 1 using DECREMENT OPERATOR
    number--; // same as number = number - 1;
    Console.WriteLine("Back again: " + number);

    // Waiting for Enter
    Console.ReadLine();
}
```

# Compound Assignment and Text

Since the + operator can be used with text, you can use the compound assignment
operator (+=) with text, too. You will probably use this frequently.

# Task

This task will get you familiar with text concatenations using compound assignment (see Figure 13-4).

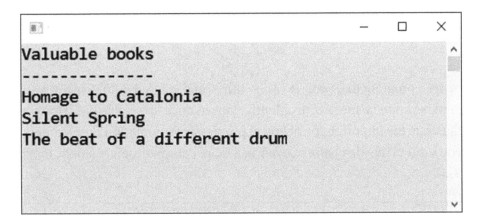

***Figure 13-4.*** *Text concatenations using compound assignment*

# Solution

Here is the code:

```
static void Main(string[] args)
{
    // Initial value (empty text)
    string books = "";

    // Appending
    books += "Homage to Catalonia" + Environment.NewLine;
    books += "Silent Spring" + Environment.NewLine;
    books += "The beat of a different drum" + Environment.NewLine;

    // Output
    Console.WriteLine("Valuable books");
    Console.WriteLine("--------------");
    Console.WriteLine(books);

    // Waiting for Enter
    Console.ReadLine();
}
```

# Progressive Summation

Progressive summation is an important principle of summing a large number of values. It means summing them not all at once in a single statement but summing them one by one, progressively accumulating intermediate results in a special variable.

## Task

You will write a program that progressively sums three entered numbers. Sure, summing three numbers would be more conveniently done at once in a single line. However, I want to illustrate the important principle of progressive summation on a simple example and get you used to the idea before covering a more complex topic, namely, loops (see Figure 13-5).

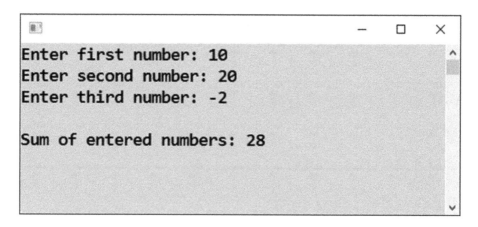

*Figure 13-5.*  *Progressively summing three entered numbers*

## Solution

Here is the code:

```
static void Main(string[] args)
{
    // Preparation - variable to accumulate intemediate result
    int sum = 0;

    // Input - 1. number
    Console.Write("Enter first number: ");
```

```
string input = Console.ReadLine();
int number = Convert.ToInt32(input);

// Adding first number to intermediate result
sum += number;

// Input - 2. number
Console.Write("Enter second number: ");
input = Console.ReadLine();
number = Convert.ToInt32(input);

// Adding second number to intermediate result
sum += number;

// Input - 3. number
Console.Write("Enter third number: ");
input = Console.ReadLine();
number = Convert.ToInt32(input);

// Adding third number to intermediate result
sum += number;

// Output
Console.WriteLine();
Console.WriteLine("Sum of entered numbers: " + sum);

// Waiting for Enter
Console.ReadLine();
}
```

# Multiple Text Join

Again, since the + operator can be used with text, too, you can extend the principle of progressive summation to text. In this context, it may rather be called *progressive accumulation*.

# Task

You will write a program that progressively accumulates names entered by the user. It will be interesting to make two accumulations; the first one is in the original order, and the second one is in the reverse order.

For simplicity, you will work with three values only (see Figure 13-6).

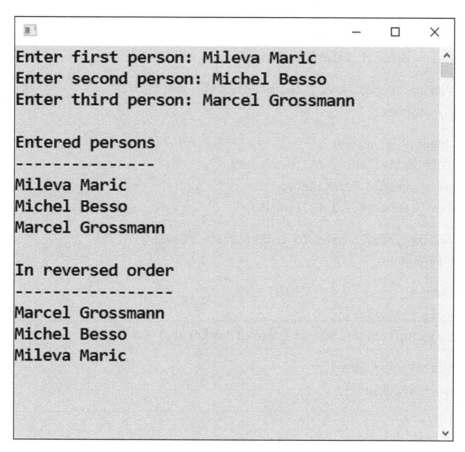

*Figure 13-6.* *Progressively accumulating names*

# Solution

Here is the code:

```
static void Main(string[] args)
{
    // Preparation - variables to accumulate intermediate results
    string inOriginalOrder = "";
    string inReversedOrder = "";

    // Input of the first person
    Console.Write("Enter first person: ");
    string person = Console.ReadLine();

    // Appending the first person to intermediate result
    inOriginalOrder += person + Environment.NewLine;
    inReversedOrder = person + Environment.NewLine + inReversedOrder;

    // Input of the second person
    Console.Write("Enter second person: ");
    person = Console.ReadLine();

    // Appending the second person to intermediate result
    inOriginalOrder += person + Environment.NewLine;
    inReversedOrder = person + Environment.NewLine + inReversedOrder;

    // Input of the third person
    Console.Write("Enter third person: ");
    person = Console.ReadLine();

    // Appending the third person to intermediate result
    inOriginalOrder += person + Environment.NewLine;
    inReversedOrder = person + Environment.NewLine + inReversedOrder;

    // Output
    Console.WriteLine();
    Console.WriteLine("Entered persons");
    Console.WriteLine("---------------");
    Console.WriteLine(inOriginalOrder);
```

```
Console.WriteLine("In reversed order");
Console.WriteLine("----------------");
Console.WriteLine(inReversedOrder);

// Waiting for Enter
Console.ReadLine();
}
```

## Note

It is interesting to note that when joining the people's names in reverse order, the compound assignment is of no help.

# Summary

The central topic of this chapter has been the accumulation of values in the same variable. Contrary to the programs so far, the programs here were repeatedly changing the value of a variable, usually using its original value, and modifying it somehow. Specifically, you studied the following:

- Statements such as `variable = variable + change;` that take the present value of `variable`, add `change` to it, and store the result as a new value of `variable`

- Compound assignments such as `variable += change;`, which are short equivalents of previous statements

- Compound assignments with other arithmetic operations: `-=, *=, /=`

- Compound assignments with text (only `+=`)

- Incrementing (adding 1) and decrementing (subtracting 1) variables using the super-short notation of `variable++;` and `variable--;`

At the end of the chapter, you got acquainted with the principle of progressive summation (and progressive accumulation), which means summing numbers one by one while storing intermediate results in a special variable. This principle is mostly used when summing a large number of values, and you will appreciate its extreme importance when studying loops later in this book.

# PART III

# Conditionals

# CHAPTER 14

# Essential Tools

You have already completed two parts of this book. In the next two parts, you will learn about more complicated topics, such as dealing with conditions and loops. So that you properly understand these topics, in this chapter I will cover some tools that can be of great help to you in your programming.

## IntelliSense

You know the first tool I will cover: Visual Studio IntelliSense. Whenever you start typing anything, Visual Studio immediately offers you options for completing the text. When you choose one of the options, the development environment shows you further details about the option in a tooltip—what the option does, what parameters it requires, and so on.

I am covering IntelliSense in this chapter because it is often underused by beginning programmers. I recommend you get used to completing virtually every word you type using IntelliSense. You will spare yourself of a huge number of typos.

## Exploring the Possibilities

Using IntelliSense is also a way to explore all the possibilities that every contemporary computing platform offers.

In former days, you had to study the possibilities in manuals or books. Some of them were capable enough to cover almost all the questions a programmer had. Today, however, there are so many possibilities that even a 1,000-page book cannot show them all.

You still need books (definitely this one!) to give you reliable and systematic instruction so you can understand the principles, but you will probably want to explore further possibilities not mentioned there. IntelliSense is a tool that can show you many of them.

179

© Radek Vystavěl 2017
R. Vystavěl, *C# Programming for Absolute Beginners*, https://doi.org/10.1007/978-1-4842-3318-4_14

# Examples

Are you looking for possibilities of how you can manipulate text? Create a variable of the `string` type and enter its name followed by a dot (see Figure 14-1).

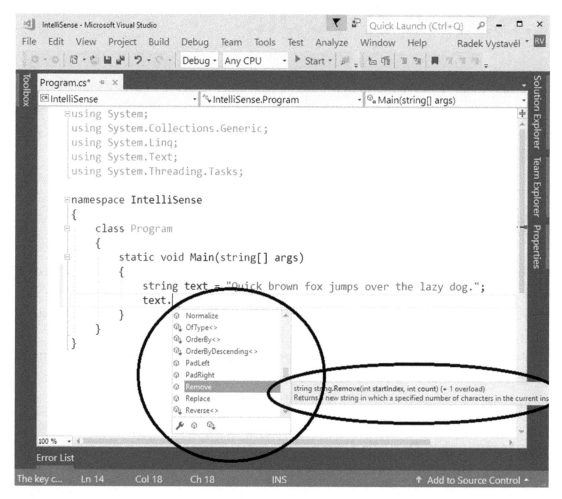

***Figure 14-1.***  *Entering a variable name and a dot*

You can find even more possibilities when you directly enter string followed by a dot (see Figure 14-2).

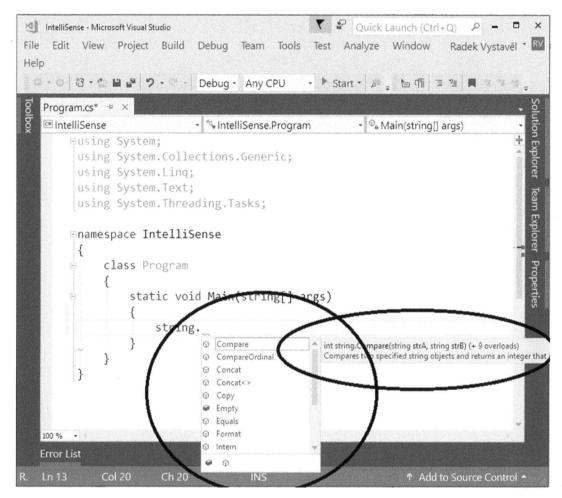

*Figure 14-2. Entering a data type and a dot*

Are you looking for actions you can perform with dates? Enter the DateTime variable and then a dot (see Figure 14-3).

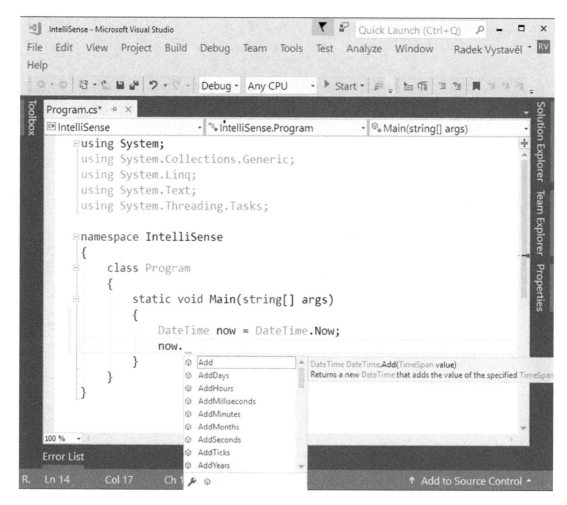

*Figure 14-3.* *Entering DateTime and a dot*

Like with text, you can enter DateTime and a dot and get some tips on what might be useful to use (see Figure 14-4).

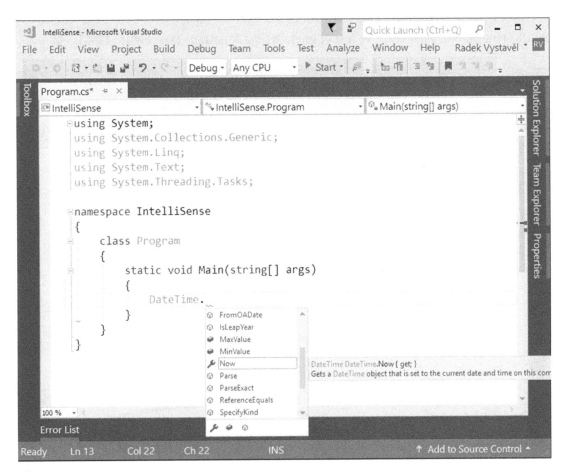

***Figure 14-4.*** *Getting some tips from IntelliSense*

## Note

The list of possibilities that IntelliSense offers you can be narrowed down using the icons at the bottom of the list. Click an appropriate icon if you want to see just properties, just methods, and so on.

## Keyboard Shortcuts

It happens sometimes that you do something and IntelliSense disappears. In this case, you may find Ctrl+J or other keyboard shortcuts useful. To get a list of them, in Visual Studio's menu bar, select Edit ➤ IntelliSense ➤ List Members (see Figure 14-5).

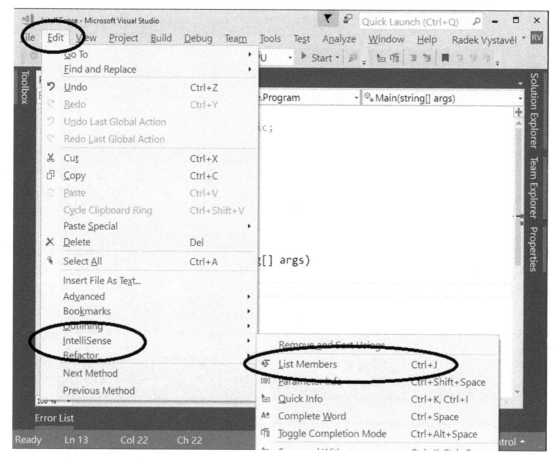

*Figure 14-5.* *Shortcut for List Members*

## Documentation

IntelliSense can give you many tips. It can also show you the basic usage of the feature you search for. However, the place where you can find all the detailed information is the online documentation.

# MSDN Portal

The Microsoft Developer Network (MSDN) at `http://msdn.microsoft.com/library` is the best place to start looking for anything concerning C# and other Microsoft technologies (see Figure 14-6).

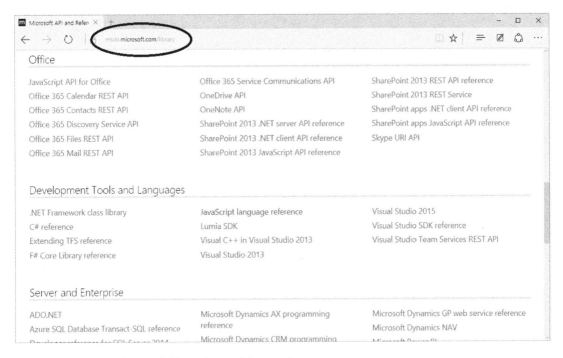

***Figure 14-6.***  *Microsoft Developer Network*

# Search

You can work with the MSDN portal using the links on the home page. However, more frequently you are going to search for specific things. In the upper-right corner of the home page, you'll see a search text field that you can bring into view by clicking the magnifying glass icon.

For example, enter **Console class** in the text field and press the Enter key (see Figure 14-7).

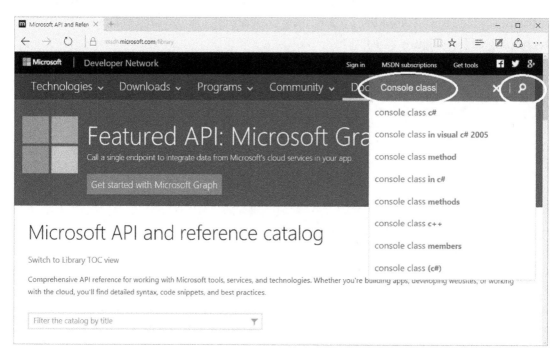

***Figure 14-7.***  *Searching for "Console class"*

The link you are interested in is often the first one returned (see Figure 14-8).

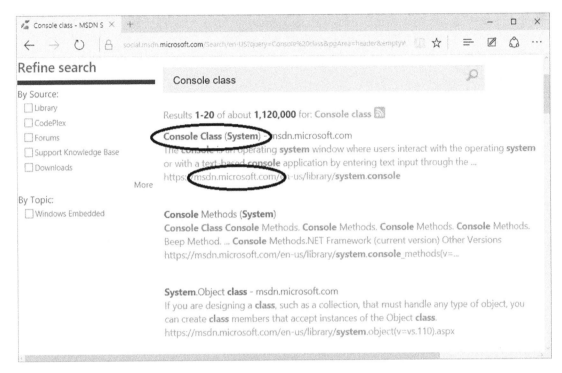

***Figure 14-8.*** *Viewing documentation for "Console class"*

In the search results, always note what web site is featured. For example, `http://msdn.microsoft.com` is on MSDN, and `http://stackoverflow.com` is a well-known forum about programming.

# Specific Class Page

After clicking the correct link, you will find all the things about a specific class, such as `Console` in this example.

You'll see a Properties list (see Figure 14-9), Actions list, Methods list, and so on.

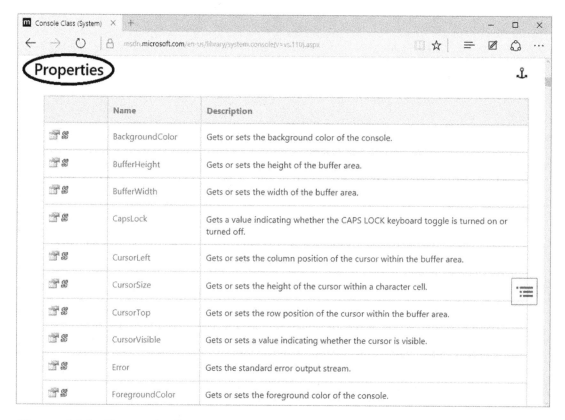

*Figure 14-9.* *Properties list*

When I am getting acquainted with some class I do not know yet, I usually look for a "Remarks" section, which covers basic information about the class usage and entry points to further details (see Figure 14-10).

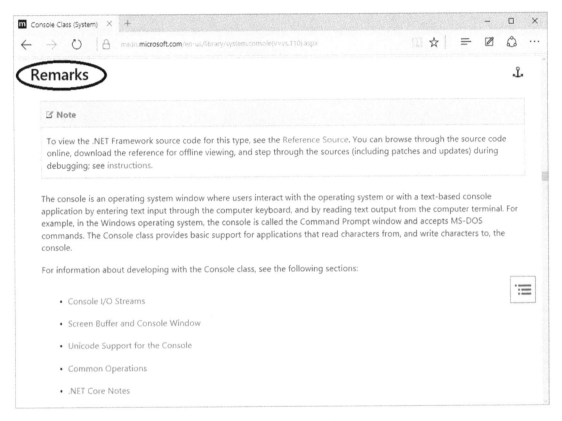

*Figure 14-10.* *Getting more details in the Remarks section*

## Common Search

To conclude this section about documentation, note that you can perform your searches outside of the MSDN portal, too. Simply use your favorite web browser to search.

However, contrary to an MSDN search, a common search displays irrelevant results more frequently. To compensate for this, you can refine your query using the programming language name, such as entering **Console class C#** in your favorite web browser's search field.

# Debugging Tools

Besides IntelliSense and documentation, there are other tools that you are going to find helpful. Specifically, you can use debugging tools that allow you to look inside a computer, so to speak. You can use them to see how the computer executes individual commands, what values are stored in memory, and so on.

These are the tools you are going to study now. Originally they were developed to facilitate program debugging, in other words, searching for and removing errors. However, they are probably even more useful as illustrative tools to facilitate your understanding of various programming constructions.

## Project

It is best to try all the tools in practice, so please open the "Treating incorrect input" project in Visual Studio from Chapter 8. The program adds two numbers and treats possible input errors using try-catch.

## Stepping Through the Code

A computer works so fast that it is impossible to follow it with its gigahertz speed. That is why it's often helpful to *step through* the code, which forces the computer to execute one statement at a time, upon your command.

Go to your opened "Treating incorrect input" project and launch it using the F10 key instead of the usual F5. Of course, selecting Debug ➤ Step Over menu does the same thing (see Figure 14-11).

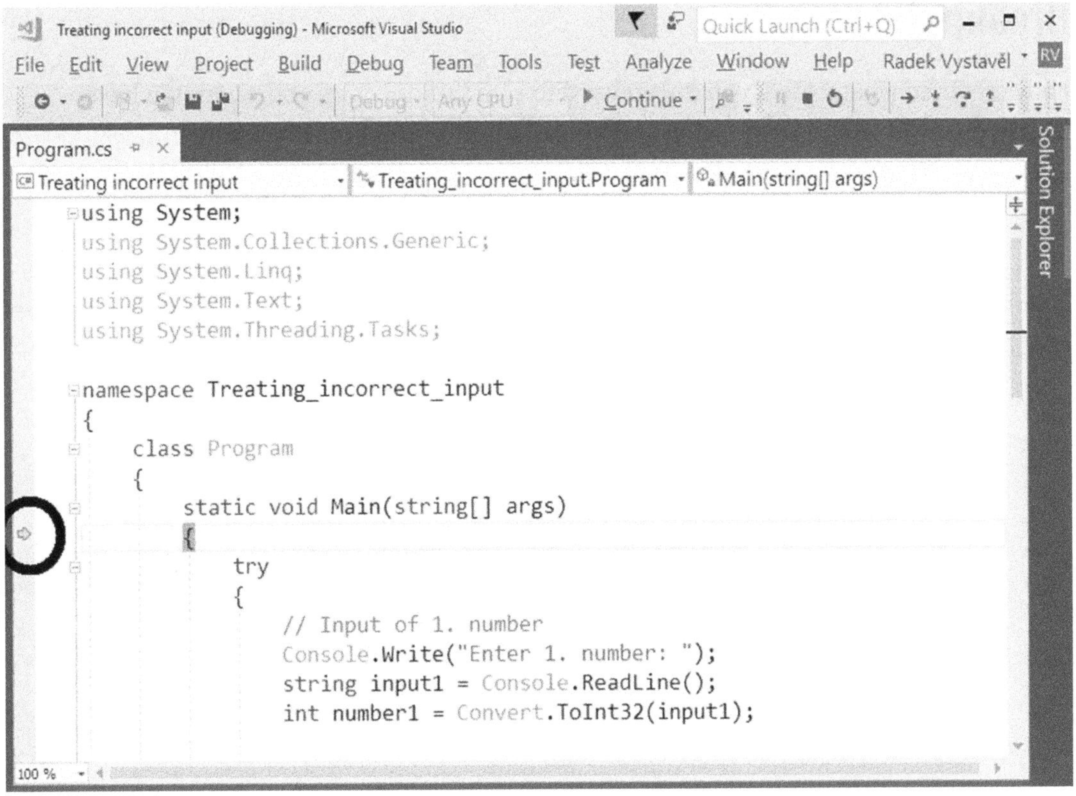

*Figure 14-11.  Launching a program using the F10 key*

The individual program statements are now being executed one at a time whenever you press F10. All the while, using a yellow arrow and yellow background, the development environment denotes the statement that is to be executed in the next step.

Now just play with the stepping. Try the case when the user enters correct data and also the case of wrong input. The IDE will show you how try-catch or anything else works. This allows you to see how the program runs with your own eyes.

## Terminate Stepping

When you find what you were looking for, you do not have to step through the program to the last statement. There are other choices.

- Using the F5 key (or Debug ➤ Continue), you can continue the regular program execution (no stepping).

- Using the Shift+F5 key (or Debug ➤ Stop Debugging), you can terminate program execution.

# Breakpoints

I have covered what to do if you do not want to step through your code after you have
passed the point you are interested in. There is another situation. Say you do not want to do
any stepping before you get to the place of interest. In that case, you can use a *breakpoint*.

Click the statement where the computer is to stop and press F9 (alternatively, right-
click and choose Breakpoint ➤ Insert Breakpoint). The fact a breakpoint has been placed
is indicated with a dark red background and a dark red bullet at the beginning of the line
(see Figure 14-12).

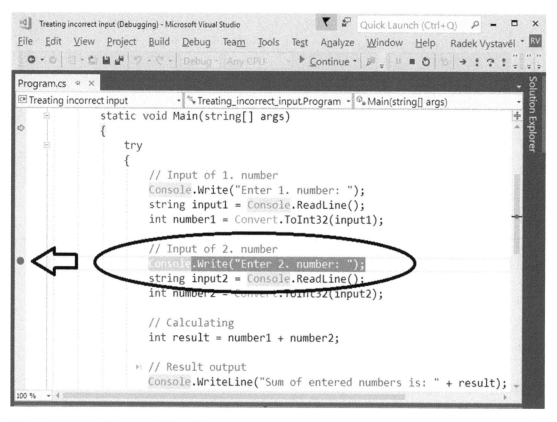

*Figure 14-12.  Inserted breakpoint*

## Using a Breakpoint

If your program is still running from the previous exercise, terminate it by using the Shift+F5 key combination. Now launch the program the regular way, in other words, using the F5 key. It will run normally, and it will stop when it reaches the breakpoint. Visual Studio pops up in front of the program's window.

After that, you can step through the code or just look at something and use the F5 key to run your program further until its end or until the next breakpoint.

## Removing a Breakpoint

To remove a breakpoint that you do not need any longer, press F9 again on a particular line, or right-click choose Breakpoint ➤ Delete Breakpoint from the context menu.

## Memory Inspection

Whenever your program is suspended (from a breakpoint, stepping, and so on), you can inspect the memory that is available to your program and explore the values of individual variables.

To facilitate memory inspection, Visual Studio shows the Autos, Locals, and Watch panes at the bottom of its window. If those panes are not there, you can display them using the Debug ➤ Windows menu.

While the Autos and Locals panes automatically select the variables to display, the Watch pane is populated manually according to what you want to see. You can enter a particular variable's name in the pane, or you can right-click the variable in the code and select Add Watch from the context menu (see Figure 14-13).

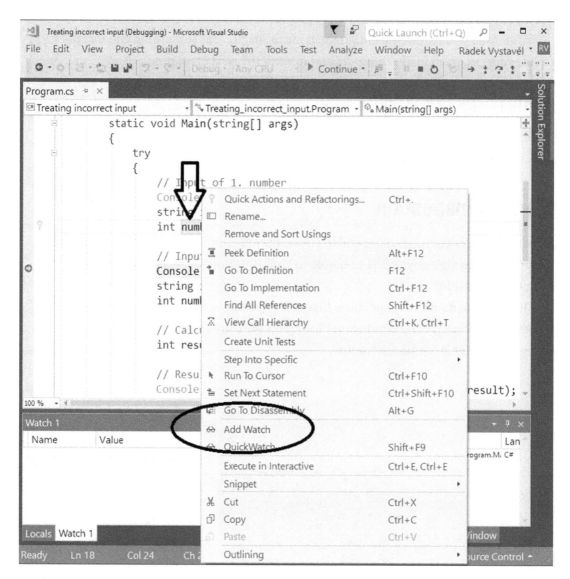

***Figure 14-13.*** *Selecting Add Watch*

The current value of the selected variable appears in the Watch window (see Figure 14-14).

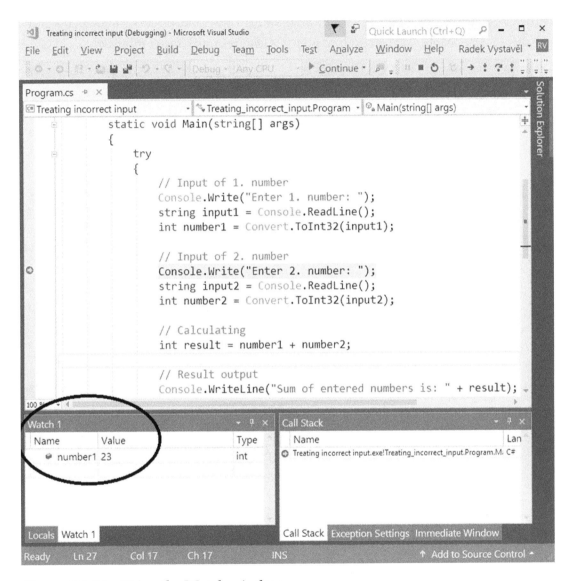

***Figure 14-14.***   *Using the Watch window*

# C# Interactive

The last tool to help you that I will mention here enables you to study C# statements in interactive mode.

# What Is It?

Up to now, you have always had to write a program with several statements and then launch it to see it in action. The interactive mode allows you to enter individual C# statements and run them immediately. You can explore some C# features much faster this way.

# How to Launch It?

You can start the interactive mode by selecting View ➤ Other Windows ➤ C# Interactive (see Figure 14-15). You do not even need to have a project created/opened.

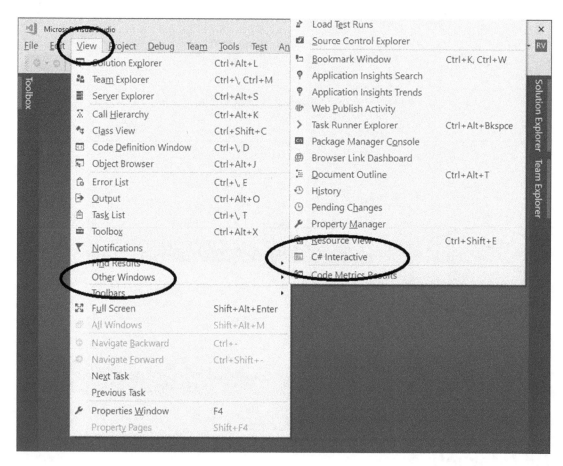

*Figure 14-15.* *Switching to interactive mode*

Figure 14-16 shows an example interactive session—I have declared a numeric variable, augmented it by ten, and displayed its value.

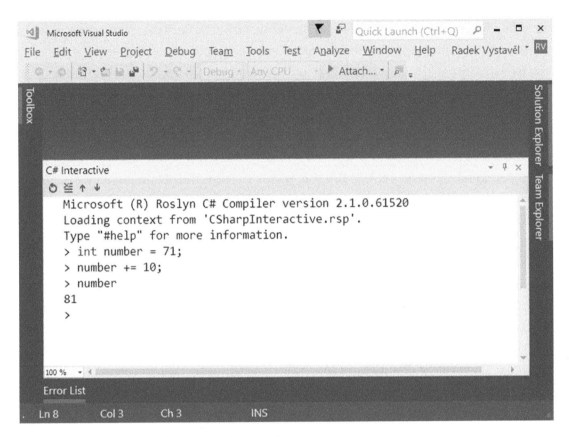

***Figure 14-16.*** *Example interactive session*

## Notes

Note the following:

- If you need to enter a multiline statement, you can terminate lines with Shift+Enter instead of simply Enter.

- Using #help displays concise information about how to work with the interactive mode.

# Summary

This chapter introduced you to the tooling that you can use in your programming, including IntelliSense, the documentation, debugging tools, and the interactive mode.

IntelliSense shows a list of available possibilities and corresponding tooltips when you type in the Visual Studio editor. You already know how to use it. Here I introduced IntelliSense as a way of exploring the huge C# universe. For example, if you want to manipulate text and you do not know precisely how a corresponding method is called, you can append a `string` variable with a dot and browse through the possibilities. You can also append the type's name with a dot to get still more possibilities.

You learned about the MSDN web site, which contains the documentation for all Microsoft programming technologies, including the C# language and the .NET platform. You usually perform full-text searches on this web site, which also includes links to a big programming forum called Stack Overflow.

In the chapter, I uncovered some debugging tools, which allow you to see "inside the computer." You can watch how individual statements are executed, check the variable values, and so on. Specifically, you learned how to step through your code, set breakpoints, and inspect the memory.

The interactive mode is a way to quickly enter C# statements and see what they do. It is a fine tool to explore new features.

# CHAPTER 15

# Getting Started with Conditions

Up to now, a program's statements have always been executed from the beginning to the end regardless of anything else, simply when their turn came. In this chapter, the whole new world will start to unveil itself because you will learn about the *conditional execution* of program statements. This means you will work with statements that may or may not execute depending on whether some *condition* is fulfilled.

## Password Input

Your first program with conditions will evaluate a password. The user may or may not be allowed to enter the system depending on whether they have entered the correct password.

## Task

You will write a program that prompts the user to enter a password and then evaluates whether the entered password is correct. For the sake of simplicity, the correct password will be specified directly in the code (see Figure 15-1 and Figure 15-2).

© Radek Vystavěl 2017
R. Vystavěl, *C# Programming for Absolute Beginners*, https://doi.org/10.1007/978-1-4842-3318-4_15

*Figure 15-1.* *Incorrect password*

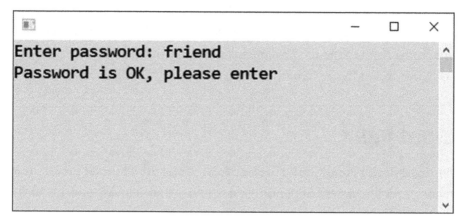

*Figure 15-2.* *Correct password*

# Analysis

Let's look at this program in more detail.

## The Program

In this program, some activity is performed when both passwords (the entered one and the stored one) agree, and a different activity is performed when they disagree. In this case, you either allow or refuse the user with an appropriate message (see Figure 15-3).

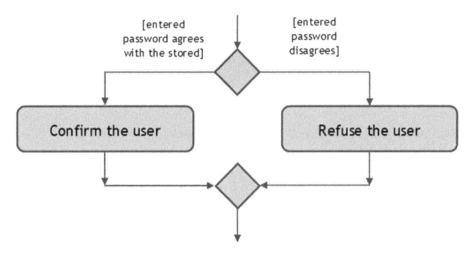

***Figure 15-3.*** *The program flow*

## Program Branching

Generally, *program branching* means taking different paths depending on the fulfillment of a condition (see Figure 15-4).

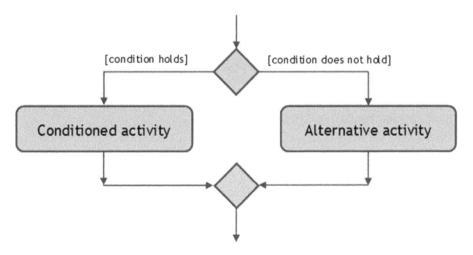

***Figure 15-4.*** *Branching*

## Syntax

For branching, C# uses the `if-else` construction shown here:

```
if (condition)
{
  Statements to perform when the condition holds
}
else
{
  Statements to perform otherwise
}
```

## Solution

Here is the code:

```
static void Main(string[] args)
{
    // Input
    Console.Write("Enter password: ");
    string enteredPassword = Console.ReadLine();

    // Password check
    if (enteredPassword == "friend")
    {
        Console.WriteLine("Password is OK, please enter");
    }
    else
    {
        Console.WriteLine("Incorrect password");
    }

    // Waiting for Enter
    Console.ReadLine();
}
```

# Discussion

To formulate the condition, I have used an equality test, which is entered using a couple of equal signs. If the compared values are the same, the test evaluates to true, the condition is considered fulfilled, and the statements in the if branch are executed. If the compared values are different, the test evaluates to false, the condition is considered not fulfilled, and the statements in the else branch are executed.

## Test

Now you can check how the program executes! Besides doing an ordinary program run, you can also step through the code, as you learned in the previous chapter.

# Reversed Condition

So that you get more familiar with conditions, it is useful to see them from different perspectives. Staying with the password issue, let's view it in another way.

# Task

The task now is to solve the previous exercise alternatively, namely, with the condition reversed. In other words, you will test for inequality instead of equality.

# Solution

Here is the code:

```
static void Main(string[] args)
{
    // Correct password
    string correctPassword = "friend";

    // Input
    Console.Write("Enter password: ");
    string enteredPassword = Console.ReadLine();
```

```
    // Password check
    if (enteredPassword != correctPassword)
    {
        Console.WriteLine("Incorrect password");
    }
    else
    {
        Console.WriteLine("Password is OK, please enter");
    }

    // Waiting for Enter
    Console.ReadLine();
}
```

## Discussion

In this exercise, I have used an inequality test, which is typed using an exclamation mark followed by an equal sign. The test returns true when the compared values **disagree**.

## Length Check

While two pieces of text can only be compared to find out if they are the same or different, two numbers can also be compared to figure out which one is longer (or shorter). Let's take a look.

## Task

In this section, you will study number comparisons in a program that evaluates whether the entered text is at most four characters long (see Figures 15-5 and 15-6).

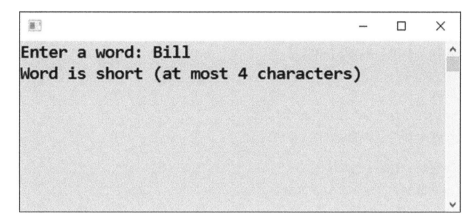

**Figure 15-5.** *Short text*

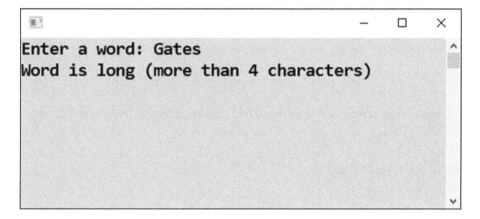

**Figure 15-6.** *Long text*

## Solution

Presumably, you should determine the number of characters of the entered text and compare it to the number 4. You learned how to determine the number of characters of text—using its Length property—in Chapter 7 (the program was "Texts as objects"). Anyway, if you do not remember the name of the property, you can add a dot to the end of a text variable and browse through the IntelliSense possibilities to see what might be appropriate, as covered in the previous chapter.

Here is the code:

```
static void Main(string[] args)
{
    // Input
    Console.Write("Enter a word: ");
    string word = Console.ReadLine();

    // Determining length
    int wordLength = word.Length;

    // Checking length
    if (wordLength <= 4)
    {
        Console.WriteLine("Word is short (at most 4 characters)");
    }
    else
    {
        Console.WriteLine("Word is long (more than 4 characters)");
    }

    // Waiting for Enter
    Console.ReadLine();
}
```

## Note

I have used a less-than-or-equal-to operator in this solution, which looks like this: <=.

# Positive Numbers

In this section, you will get some more practice with number comparisons.

# Task

You will write a program that evaluates whether the number entered by the user is positive or not (see Figures 15-7 and 15-8).

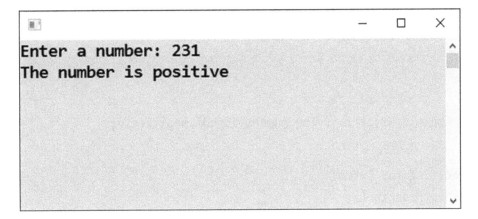

***Figure 15-7.*** *It's positive.*

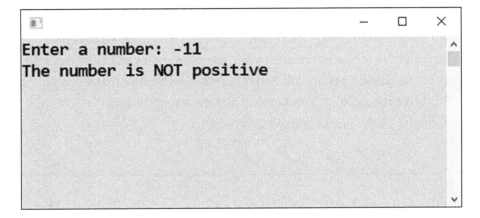

***Figure 15-8.*** *It's not positive.*

## Solution

Here is the code:

```
static void Main(string[] args)
{
    // Input
    Console.Write("Enter a number: ");
    string input = Console.ReadLine();
    int number = Convert.ToInt32(input);

    // Evaluation
    if (number > 0)
```

```
    {
        Console.WriteLine("The number is positive");
    }
    else
    {
        Console.WriteLine("The number is NOT positive");
    }

    // Waiting for Enter
    Console.ReadLine();
}
```

## Discussion

I have used a greater-than operator to compare the entered number to zero.

What do you think the program does when the user enters zero? It checks the condition 0 > 0 and finds it is not fulfilled. Therefore, it displays that the number is not positive. This is the reason for the rather unusual message wording ("... NOT positive"), as shown in Figure 15-9. I have not used "...is negative".

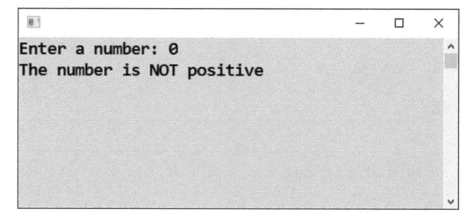

*Figure 15-9.* *Results for zero*

# Odd and Even Numbers

Let's proceed to another number comparison.

## Task

Your task now is to write a program that evaluates whether the number entered by the user is odd or even (see Figure 15-10 and Figure 15-11).

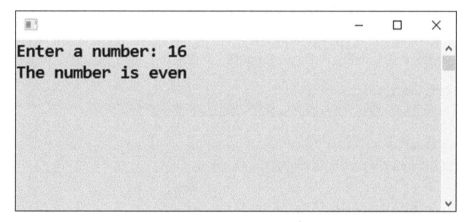

***Figure 15-10.*** *Determining even*

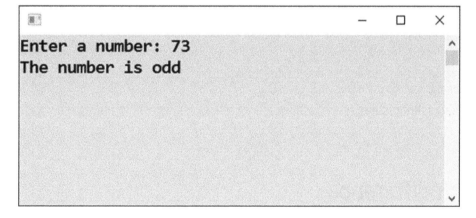

***Figure 15-11.*** *Determining odd*

## Solution

The core of the solution is to determine the remainder of dividing the entered number by 2. If the remainder is zero, the number is even. If there is some remainder, the number is odd.

Here is the code:

```
static void Main(string[] args)
{
    // Input
    Console.Write("Enter a number: ");
    string input = Console.ReadLine();
    int number = Convert.ToInt32(input);

    // Remainder calculation
    int remainderAfterDivisionByTwo = number % 2;

    // Evaluation
    if (remainderAfterDivisionByTwo == 0)
    {
        Console.WriteLine("The number is even");
    }
    else
    {
        Console.WriteLine("The number is odd");
    }

    // Waiting for Enter
    Console.ReadLine();
}
```

## Case Indifference

You already know that two pieces of text can be compared to see if they are equal or unequal. This comparison is case-sensitive. In other words, *hobbit* and *Hobbit* are considered different words. Frequently, however, you need case-insensitive comparisons, which I will show you now.

# Task

In this program, the user will enter two names, and you will evaluate whether they are the same or different, disregarding the difference between lowercase and uppercase (see Figures 15-12 and 15-13).

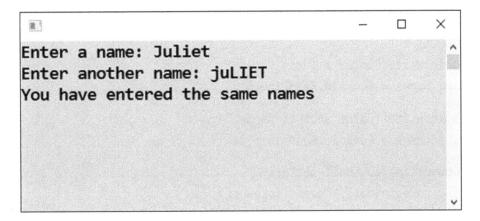

**Figure 15-12.** *The same names*

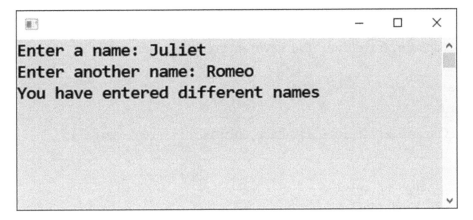

**Figure 15-13.** *Different names*

## Solution

The core of the solution is to convert both pieces of text to lowercase prior to doing the comparison. You can use the ToLower method call for that purpose.

Here is the code:

```
static void Main(string[] args)
{
    // Inputs
    Console.Write("Enter a name: ");
    string name1 = Console.ReadLine();

    Console.Write("Enter another name: ");
    string name2 = Console.ReadLine();

    // Converting to small letters
    string name1inSmall = name1.ToLower();
    string name2inSmall = name2.ToLower();

    // Evaluating
    if (name1inSmall == name2inSmall)
    {
        Console.WriteLine("You have entered the same names");
    }
    else
    {
        Console.WriteLine("You have entered different names");
    }

    // Waiting for Enter
    Console.ReadLine();
}
```

## Without Braces

C# allows you to omit the braces surrounding the if and else branches if the branch contains just a single statement. Generally, I do not recommend this practice because it can be misleading. I will show this to you now just so that you are aware of it.

# Task

You will solve the previous exercise again, this time without braces.

# Solution

Here is the code:

```
static void Main(string[] args)
{
    // Inputs
    Console.Write("Enter a name: ");
    string name1 = Console.ReadLine();

    Console.Write("Enter another name: ");
    string name2 = Console.ReadLine();

    // Converting to small letters
    string name1inSmall = name1.ToLower();
    string name2inSmall = name2.ToLower();

    // Evaluating
    // BRANCHES NOT DELIMITED BY BRACES (CURLY BRACKETS)
    if (name1inSmall == name2inSmall)
        Console.WriteLine("You have entered the same names");
    else
        Console.WriteLine("You have entered different names");

    // Waiting for Enter
    Console.ReadLine();
}
```

# Greater of Two Numbers

A frequent task of a programmer is to find which of two numbers is greater (or smaller, analogously).

# Task

Your task now is to write a program that asks the user for two numbers and then says which of the two numbers is greater (see Figure 15-14).

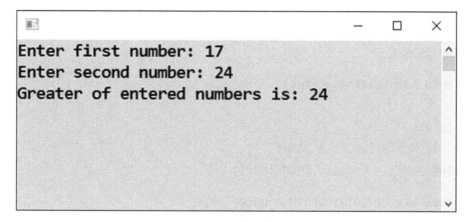

```
Enter first number: 17
Enter second number: 24
Greater of entered numbers is: 24
```

***Figure 15-14.***  *Determining which number is greater*

# Solution

Here is the code:

```
static void Main(string[] args)
{
    // Inputs
    Console.Write("Enter first number: ");
    string input1 = Console.ReadLine();
    int number1 = Convert.ToInt32(input1);

    Console.Write("Enter second number: ");
    string input2 = Console.ReadLine();
    int number2 = Convert.ToInt32(input2);

    // Evaluating
    int greater;
    if (number1 > number2)
    {
        greater = number1;
    }
```

```
else
{
    greater = number2;
}

// Output
Console.WriteLine("Greater of entered numbers is: " + greater);

// Waiting for Enter
Console.ReadLine();
}
```

# Without the else Branch

In previous exercises, you always had two branches—the if branch and the else branch. In other words, you were always in an either-or situation. It is important to note, however, that the else branch can be omitted if you want. This means if a condition is fulfilled, you do something, and if it is not fulfilled, you simply do nothing. Take a look!

## Task

In the previous exercise, you set the greater variable either to the first value or to the second value.

Now you will solve the same task in a different way. First you will set the greater variable directly to the first value, and then if the second one is greater, you will change the final result.

## Solution

Here is the code:

```
static void Main(string[] args)
{
    // Inputs
    Console.Write("Enter first number: ");
    string input1 = Console.ReadLine();
```

```
    int number1 = Convert.ToInt32(input1);

    Console.Write("Enter second number: ");
    string input2 = Console.ReadLine();
    int number2 = Convert.ToInt32(input2);

    // Evaluating
    int greater = number1;
    if (number2 > greater)
    {
        greater = number2;
    }

    // Output
    Console.WriteLine("Greater of entered numbers is: " + greater);

    // Waiting for Enter
    Console.ReadLine();
}
```

# Using a Built-in Function

Frequently in this book, I show you things from different angles. I strongly believe this promotes your understanding. For the current problem of finding the greater value of two, I will show you a third way to solve it. The task is so frequent, in fact, that there is a convenient built-in function for it.

# Task

You will solve the previous exercise using the built-in function `Math.Max`.

# Solution

Here is the code:

```
static void Main(string[] args)
{
    // Inputs
    Console.Write("Enter first number: ");
    string input1 = Console.ReadLine();
    int number1 = Convert.ToInt32(input1);

    Console.Write("Enter second number: ");
    string input2 = Console.ReadLine();
    int number2 = Convert.ToInt32(input2);

    // Evaluating
    int greater = Math.Max(number1, number2);

    // Output
    Console.WriteLine("Greater of entered numbers is: " + greater);

    // Waiting for Enter
    Console.ReadLine();
}
```

# Summary

In this chapter, you started studying the conditional execution of program statements, which means that the execution or nonexecution of one or more statements can be conditioned by some test. You saw the following examples of tests:

- Testing the equality of two pieces of text or two numbers with the == operator

- Testing the inequality of two pieces of text or two numbers with the != operator

- Testing whether a number is greater (or less) than another number with the > (or <) operator

The last test can be extended to "greater than or equal to" (or "less than or equal to") with the >= (or <=) operator.

To use conditional execution in your code, you learned about the if-else construct. This consists of a condition and two branches. If the condition is evaluated to be true (fulfilled), the statements in the if branch are executed. If the condition is evaluated to be false (not fulfilled), the statements in the else branch are executed.

You learned that if a branch consists of a single statement, C# syntax allows you to omit the braces surrounding the branch, though I discourage you from doing that because people frequently forget to include the braces later when they extend a branch to several statements.

More important, you learned that the else branch can be omitted if you want. This means there is no alternative action—nothing is done when the condition is not fulfilled.

As a bonus, you learned about the useful built-in function Math.Max. (You can probably guess that there is a similar function called Math.Min.)

# CHAPTER 16

# Practical Conditions

In the previous chapter, you learned about the conditional execution of a program's statements. In this chapter, you will deepen your knowledge of this topic. I will show you how to use conditions and branching on several simple tasks that you will encounter sooner or later in your programming career.

## Appending Extension

Sometimes you want to ask the user about a file name, but you do not know whether the user will enter it with or without an extension.

## Task

You will write a program that appends the .png extension to the entered file name unless the extension is already part of the input (see Figures 16-1 and 16-2).

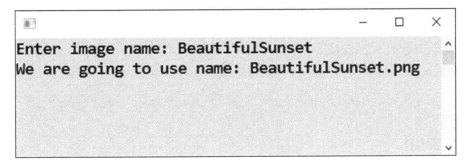

*Figure 16-1.* *Appending the .png extension*

© Radek Vystavěl 2017
R. Vystavěl, *C# Programming for Absolute Beginners*, https://doi.org/10.1007/978-1-4842-3318-4_16

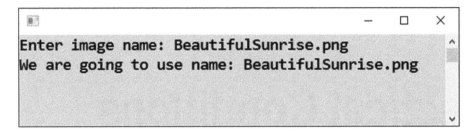

*Figure 16-2.* *Not appending the .png extension*

## Solution

Here is the code:

```
static void Main(string[] args)
{
    // Input
    Console.Write("Enter image name: ");
    string fileName = Console.ReadLine();

    // Appending extension (ONLY IN CASE OF NEED)
    if (!fileName.ToLower().EndsWith(".png"))
    {
        fileName += ".png";
    }

    // Output
    Console.WriteLine("We are going to use name: " + fileName);

    // Waiting for Enter
    Console.ReadLine();
}
```

## Discussion

Let's discuss this program a bit.

## Extension Detection

The most interesting point of the current exercise is finding out whether the entered file name ends with a particular extension.

- First, you convert the file name to lowercase so you do not have to distinguish between `.png` and `.PNG`.

- You use the method `EndsWith` to find whether the text ends or does not end with something specific. In this case, the method call returns `true` if the text ends with `.png`. Otherwise, it returns `false`.

- You negate the result returned by the `EndsWith` method using the `!` operator. The exclamation mark changes `true` to `false`, and vice versa. This means you actually ask "Does the text *not* end with `.png`?" instead of "Does it end with `.png`?"

## Entering a Condition

Note that you do not always have to enter a comparison when specifying a condition. You do not always have to use "less than," for example. It is enough if the condition evaluates to a Boolean value, such as `true` or `false`.

If the condition evaluates to `true`, it is considered fulfilled, and the statements in the `if` branch are executed.

If the condition evaluates to `false`, it is considered not fulfilled, and the statements in the `else` branch are executed (or nothing is executed in the case of a missing `else` branch).

## Missing else Branch

The example program has a missing `else` branch. If the entered name ends with `.png`, the `EndsWith` method will find it and will return `true`. If you get `false`, the condition is considered not fulfilled, so the statement appending the extension will not be executed, and the entered name will remain unchanged.

## Chaining

Note the *chaining* of the `ToLower` and `EndsWith` methods. The output of the lowercase conversion is not stored in any variable. Instead, it serves as input for the next method in the chain, in other words, `EndsWith`.

# Head and Tail

Let's do some more exercises concerning conditions.

## Task

You will write a program that throws a coin once (see Figure 16-3).

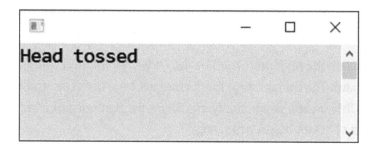

*Figure 16-3.* *Throwing a coin*

## Solution

The core of the solution is to generate a random number—zero or one—and convert it to heads or tails subsequently.

Here is the code:

```
static void Main(string[] args)
{
    // Random number generator
    Random randomNumbers = new Random();

    // Random number 0/1 and its transformation
    int randomNumber = randomNumbers.Next(0, 1 + 1);
    if (randomNumber == 0)
    {
        Console.WriteLine("Head tossed");
    }
    else
    {
```

```
        Console.WriteLine("Tail tossed");
    }

    // Waiting for Enter
    Console.ReadLine();
}
```

## Discussion

I just want to remind you that the Next method requires the upper bound of a random number range to be specified already augmented by 1. That is why you wrote 1+1 in the previous program. Of course, you could also have written 2 directly, but 1+1 seems to me more logical, stating 1 as the upper bound and adding the (strangely) required 1.

# Deadline Check

"Never trust the user," as the old saying goes. This means you as a programmer always have to check user-entered data in production software.

You need to check the user data usually not because of malicious use because 99.9 percent of your users do not have any intention to abuse your software. Users simply make mistakes. That is why you should check their input and prompt them to correct it.

So, now you will learn how to implement some input checking.

## Task

You will write a program that prompts the user to enter an order deadline and presents a warning if the user enters a date in the past (see Figure 16-4).

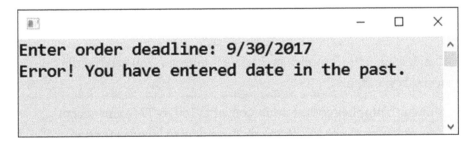

***Figure 16-4.*** *Checking a date*

# Solution

Here is the code:

```
static void Main(string[] args)
{
    // Input
    Console.Write("Enter order deadline: ");
    string input = Console.ReadLine();
    DateTime enteredDeadline = Convert.ToDateTime(input);

    // Checking entered value
    DateTime today = DateTime.Today;
    if (enteredDeadline < today)
    {
        Console.WriteLine("Error! You have entered date in the past.");
    }
    else
    {
        Console.WriteLine("Deadline accepted.");
    }

    // Waiting for Enter
    Console.ReadLine();
}
```

## Discussion

Note the following:

- To convert a date entered in text form into the DateTime object, you use the Convert.ToDateTime method call.

- Conversion fails if a nonexistent date is entered. You can handle this using try-catch.

- Similar to number conversions, Convert.ToDateTime can accept a second parameter specifying the language to be used for the conversion.

# Invoice Date Check

Let's do one more exercise for checking user-entered data.

## Task

Value-added tax (VAT) regulations in my country require that the date an invoice is issued cannot precede the date of payment, and at the same time, it cannot be later than 15 days after the payment.

The current task is to perform both checks (see Figure 16-5, Figure 16-6, and Figure 16-7).

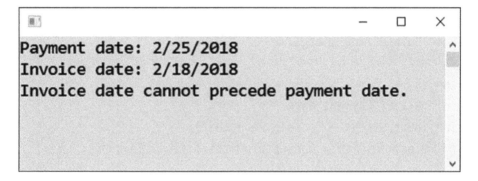

***Figure 16-5.*** *Date too early*

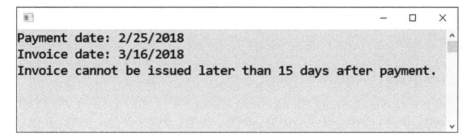

***Figure 16-6.*** *Date too late*

*Figure 16-7.* *Dates accepted*

## Solution

Here is the solution:

```
static void Main(string[] args)
{
    // Inputs
    Console.Write("Payment date: ");
    string inputPayment = Console.ReadLine();
    DateTime paymentDate = Convert.ToDateTime(inputPayment);

    Console.Write("Invoice date: ");
    string inputInvoice = Console.ReadLine();
    DateTime invoiceDate = Convert.ToDateTime(inputInvoice);

    // Checking
    bool ok = true;
    if (invoiceDate < paymentDate)
    {
        Console.WriteLine("Invoice date cannot precede payment date.");
        ok = false;
    }
    if (invoiceDate > paymentDate.AddDays(15))
    {
        Console.WriteLine("Invoice cannot be issued later than 15 days
        after payment.");
        ok = false;
    }
```

```
    if (ok)
    {
        Console.WriteLine("Dates accepted.");
    }

    // Waiting for Enter
    Console.ReadLine();
}
```

## Discussion

You are using a helper variable called ok in this solution. The variable monitors whether everything is OK. At first, you set it to true. If any of the performed checks fail, you toggle the value to false. If the variable stays true after both checks, you know everything is OK, and a confirming message is displayed to the user.

# Spanish Day of Week

Now you will learn how to split the code's execution into multiple branches.

## Task

You will write a program that displays the Spanish version of the day of week (lunes, martes, miércoles, and so on) for a date entered by the user (see Figure 16-8).

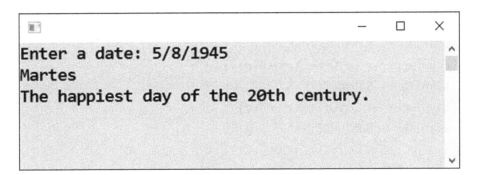

*Figure 16-8.* *Displaying days in Spanish*

# Solution

You can find the day of the week using the DayOfWeek property of the DateTime object. The conversion to Spanish can be made using a series of conditions.

Here is the code:

```
static void Main(string[] args)
{
    // Input
    Console.Write("Enter a date: ");
    string input = Console.ReadLine();
    DateTime enteredDate = Convert.ToDateTime(input);

    // Finding day of week (in enumeration)
    DayOfWeek dayOfWeek = enteredDate.DayOfWeek;

    // Spanish texts
    string spanish = "";
    if (dayOfWeek == DayOfWeek.Monday)
        spanish = "Lunes";
    if (dayOfWeek == DayOfWeek.Tuesday)
        spanish = "Martes";
    if (dayOfWeek == DayOfWeek.Wednesday)
        spanish = "Miercoles";
    if (dayOfWeek == DayOfWeek.Thursday)
        spanish = "Jueves";
    if (dayOfWeek == DayOfWeek.Friday)
        spanish = "Viernes";
    if (dayOfWeek == DayOfWeek.Saturday)
        spanish = "Sábado";
    if (dayOfWeek == DayOfWeek.Sunday)
        spanish = "Domingo";

    // Output
    Console.WriteLine(spanish);
    if (enteredDate == new DateTime(1945, 5, 8))
        Console.WriteLine("The happiest day of the 20th century.");
```

```
    // Waiting for Enter
    Console.ReadLine();
}
```

## Discussion

Note the following:

- You have omitted braces surrounding individual if branches. You can do that because there is only a single statement in every branch. I normally do not do this, but in this case of many simple ifs, it seemed to me that it would make the code neater.

- Individual days of the week are members of the DayOfWeek enumeration. Visual Studio offers you the enumeration as soon as you hit the spacebar on your keyboard after entering two equal signs (see Figure 16-9). Use what Visual Studio offers!

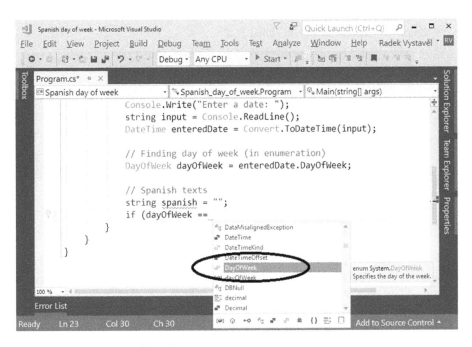

***Figure 16-9.*** *Using DayOfWeek enumeration*

# Switch Statement

For certain cases of multiple branching, there also exists a switch statement in C#. Now you will learn how to work with it.

## Task

You will solve the last task using a switch statement.

## Solution

Here is the code:

```
static void Main(string[] args)
{
    // Input
    Console.Write("Enter a date: ");
    string input = Console.ReadLine();
    DateTime enteredDate = Convert.ToDateTime(input);

    // Finding day of week (in enumeration)
    DayOfWeek dayOfWeek = enteredDate.DayOfWeek;

    // Spanish texts
    string spanish = "";
    switch (dayOfWeek)
    {
        case DayOfWeek.Monday:
            spanish = "Lunes";
            break;
        case DayOfWeek.Tuesday:
            spanish = "Martes";
            break;
        case DayOfWeek.Wednesday:
            spanish = "Miercoles";
            break;
        case DayOfWeek.Thursday:
```

```
                spanish = "Jueves";
                break;
            case DayOfWeek.Friday:
                spanish = "Viernes";
                break;
            case DayOfWeek.Saturday:
                spanish = "Sábado";
                break;
            case DayOfWeek.Sunday:
                spanish = "Domingo";
                break;
        }

        // Output
        Console.WriteLine(spanish);
        if (enteredDate == new DateTime(1945, 5, 8))
            Console.WriteLine("The happiest day of the 20th century.");

        // Waiting for Enter
        Console.ReadLine();
}
```

## Discussion

You can use the switch statement as an if-series replacement if the repeated branching is always based on the same value. This is the dayOfWeek variable's value in this case.

As to the syntax, the switch keyword is followed (in parentheses) by a variable (or expression) whose value determines which branch the execution will take. The individual branches start with the case keyword followed by a specific value of the control variable and a colon. You should terminate each branch with the break keyword.

# Summary

In this chapter, you wrote programs with conditional execution for a variety of practical tasks. Specifically, you learned the following:

- To enter conditions without any of relational operators such as <, ==, and so on. The condition simply has to evaluate to the `bool` type. It is considered fulfilled when it evaluates to `true`.

- To negate the condition using the ! operator.

- To transform random numbers into another kind of data, such as a heads/tails pair.

- To perform various checks of the user input, especially for dates.

- To branch your program into several alternative execution paths, either by using a series of `if` statements or by using `switch` statement.

# CHAPTER 17

# Compound Conditions

You have now some experience formulating conditions and using them to solve real problems. As to more complex problems, what you often need is to assemble your condition out of two or more partial conditions. This is what you will study in this chapter.

## Yes or No

Your first use of compound conditions will be to check that the user input belongs to one of the allowed alternatives.

## Task

You will write a program that checks whether the user entered *either* yes *or* no. All other inputs will be considered incorrect (see Figures 17-1 and 17-2).

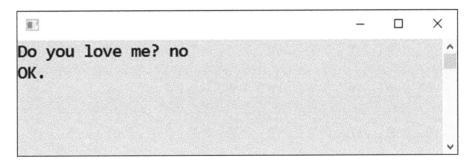

***Figure 17-1.*** *Acceptable answer but sad*

© Radek Vystavěl 2017

R. Vystavěl, *C# Programming for Absolute Beginners*, https://doi.org/10.1007/978-1-4842-3318-4_17

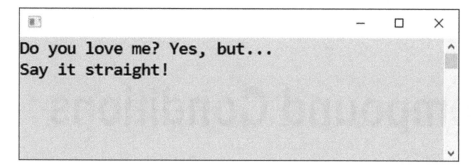

*Figure 17-2.* *Yes!*

## Solution

Here's the code:

```
static void Main(string[] args)
{
    // Input
    Console.Write("Do you love me? ");
    string input = Console.ReadLine();

    // Evaluating
    string inputInSmall = input.ToLower();
    if (inputInSmall == "yes" || inputInSmall == "no")
    {
        Console.WriteLine("OK.");
    }
    else
    {
        Console.WriteLine("Say it straight!");
    }

    // Waiting for Enter
    Console.ReadLine();
}
```

# Discussion

Note the following:

- To disregard the difference in case, you convert the input to lowercase letters.

- The condition used is a compound condition. It consists of two partial conditions connected using the conditional OR operator, which is typed as || (two vertical lines).

- The condition is fulfilled (and the `if` branch is executed) if **at least one** of the partial conditions is fulfilled. This means the user entered *either* yes *or* no. In this case, the alternatives are mutually exclusive. However, you will encounter cases when both conditions can be fulfilled simultaneously.

- The condition is not fulfilled (and the `else` branch is executed) if neither the first nor the second partial condition is fulfilled. In other words, the user entered something besides yes or no.

# Username and Password

Now you will look at partial conditions that should always be fulfilled simultaneously.

# Task

You will write a program that checks whether the user entered the correct username (Orwell) *and at the same time* the correct password (Catalonia). The username is case-insensitive, meaning it can be lowercase and uppercase (see Figures 17-3 and 17-4).

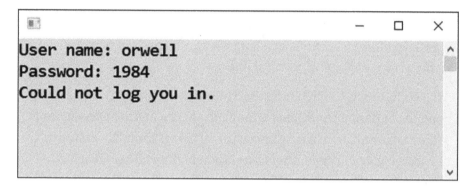

***Figure 17-3.*** *Correct username but incorrect password*

***Figure 17-4.*** *Correct username and password*

# Solution

Here is the code:

```
static void Main(string[] args)
{
    // Correct values
    string correctUsername = "Orwell";
    string correctPassword = "Catalonia";
```

```
// Inputs
Console.Write("User name: ");
string enteredUserName = Console.ReadLine();

Console.Write("Password: ");
string enteredPassword = Console.ReadLine();

// Evaluating
if (enteredUserName.ToLower() == correctUsername.ToLower() &&
    enteredPassword == correctPassword)
{
    Console.WriteLine("Thanks for your books!");
}
else
{
    Console.WriteLine("Could not log you in.");
}

// Waiting for Enter
Console.ReadLine();
}
```

## Discussion

Note the following:

- The condition used is a compound condition again. Its partial conditions are connected using the conditional AND operator, which is typed as && (two ampersands).

- The condition is fulfilled (and the if branch is executed) if *both* partial conditions are fulfilled simultaneously. This means the user has to enter both the correct username and the correct password.

- To not fulfill the condition (and thus execute the else branch), it is enough to not fulfill either one of the partial conditions.

# Two Users

You can even combine several AND and OR operators to get a really complex compound condition. Take a look!

## Task

You will modify the previous task to allow two possible users to log in. Both will have their own passwords.

## Solution

Here is the code:

```
static void Main(string[] args)
{
    // Correct values
    string correctUsername1 = "Orwell";
    string correctPassword1 = "Catalonia";

    string correctUsername2 = "Blair";
    string correctPassword2 = "1984";

    // Inputs
    Console.Write("User name: ");
    string enteredUsername = Console.ReadLine();

    Console.Write("Password: ");
    string enteredPassword = Console.ReadLine();

    // Evalulating
    if (enteredUsername.ToLower() == correctUsername1.ToLower() &&
        enteredPassword == correctPassword1 ||
        enteredUsername.ToLower() == correctUsername2.ToLower() &&
        enteredPassword == correctPassword2)
    {
        Console.WriteLine("Thanks for your books!");
    }
```

```
    else
    {
        Console.WriteLine("Could not log you in.");
    }

    // Waiting for Enter
    Console.ReadLine();
}
```

## Discussion

Note the following:

- You can combine both conditional operators: AND with OR.

- Fulfillment of the complete condition requires the user to enter the correct first username and the correct first password or the correct second username and the correct second password.

- The condition intentionally uses a *higher priority* (precedence) for the AND operator compared to the OR operator. Specifically, both potential users are evaluated first, and the partial results are ORed afterward.

- If you need a different evaluation order, just use parentheses (round brackets) similarly to mathematics.

# Precalculation of Conditions

The compound condition in the previous exercise is already quite complex. To understand this, you must concentrate on it. In similar situations, it may be better to precalculate (calculate in advance) partial conditions. This is what I am going to show you now.

# Task

The task is the same as the previous one, but the solution will be different.

# Solution

Here is the code:

```
static void Main(string[] args)
{
    // Correct values
    string correctUsername1 = "Orwell";
    string correctPassword1 = "Catalonia";

    string correctUsername2 = "Blair";
    string correctPassword2 = "1984";

    // Inputs
    Console.Write("User name: ");
    string enteredUsername = Console.ReadLine();

    Console.Write("Password: ");
    string enteredPassword = Console.ReadLine();

    // Evaluating
    bool user1ok = enteredUsername.ToLower() == correctUsername1.ToLower() &&
                enteredPassword == correctPassword1;
    bool user2ok = enteredUsername.ToLower() == correctUsername2.ToLower() &&
                enteredPassword == correctPassword2;
    if (user1ok || user2ok)
    {
        Console.WriteLine("Thanks for your books!");
    }
    else
    {
        Console.WriteLine("Could not log you in.");
    }

    // Waiting for Enter
    Console.ReadLine();
}
```

# Discussion

Note the following:

- You check both users one after another. The main condition can then be written in a clear and concise way.

- Partial conditions are precalculated into variables of type bool. When a condition is fulfilled, the corresponding variable has its value set to true.

# Yes or No Reversed

You learned about reversing conditions already in Chapter 15. In that chapter, the condition was simple. Now you will reverse a compound condition, which is a bit trickier and requires greater care.

## Task

You will return to the "Yes or No" project from the beginning of this chapter once again. For the purpose of practicing compound conditions, think about how you would reverse the original condition to swap the if and else branches.

## Solution

Here is the code:

```
static void Main(string[] args)
{
    // Input
    Console.Write("Do you love me? ");
    string input = Console.ReadLine();

    // Evaluating
    string inputInSmall = input.ToLower();
    if (inputInSmall != "yes" && inputInSmall != "no")
    {
```

```
        Console.WriteLine("Say it straight!");
    }
    else
    {
        Console.WriteLine("OK.");
    }

    // Waiting for Enter
    Console.ReadLine();
}
```

## Discussion

Note the following:

- Instead of checking the correct input, you now check the incorrect one.

- The input is incorrect when it neither equals yes nor no.

- Reversing the condition caused the OR operator to change into the AND operator. It also caused the equalities to change into inequalities.

## Grade Check

Now I would like to turn your attention to a frequent test of a number belonging to a specified set, or a specified range. The following two tasks concern this.

## Task

The user enters a grade of a student. The program will check then whether the entered number is in the set of possible values 1, 2, 3, 4, or 5 (see Figure 17-5 and Figure 17-6).

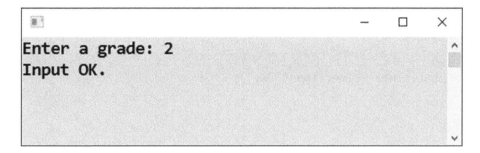

**Figure 17-5.** *Within the range*

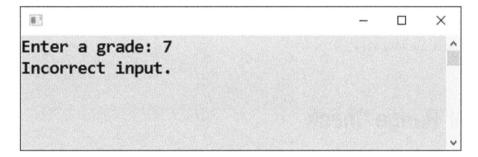

**Figure 17-6.** *Not within the range*

## Solution

The condition can be formulated enumerating the individual alternatives. For the sake of simplicity, I do not check for possible non-numeric input. You can handle this yourself using try-catch as usual.

Here is the code:

```
static void Main(string[] args)
{
    // Input
    Console.Write("Enter a grade: ");
    string input = Console.ReadLine();
    int grade = Convert.ToInt32(input);

    // Evaluating
    if (grade == 1 ||
        grade == 2 ||
        grade == 3 ||
```

```
        grade == 4 ||
        grade == 5)
    {
        Console.WriteLine("Input OK.");
    }
    else
    {
        Console.WriteLine("Incorrect input.");
    }

    // Waiting for Enter
    Console.ReadLine();
}
```

# Better Range Check

The allowed numbers (possible grades) actually constitute a range of 1 to 5 (a continuous range without gaps). In such a case, you can use a better way to check whether a number belongs to a specific range or not.

## Task

The task is to solve the previous exercise using a range check.

## Solution

A number belongs to a range given by its lower and upper bounds when it is greater than or equal to the lower bound and at the same time it is less than or equal to the upper bound.

Here is the code:

```
static void Main(string[] args)
{
    // Input
    Console.Write("Enter a grade: ");
    string input = Console.ReadLine();
    int grade = Convert.ToInt32(input);
```

```
    // Evaluating
    if (grade >= 1 && grade <= 5)
    {
        Console.WriteLine("Input OK.");
    }
    else
    {
        Console.WriteLine("Incorrect input.");
    }

    // Waiting for Enter
    Console.ReadLine();
}
```

# Summary

This chapter introduced you to the topic of compound conditions. You learned that the if statement condition can be compounded by several partial conditions joined together using conditional AND and conditional OR operators.

In C#, the AND operator is written as &&, and it evaluates to true when both partial conditions are fulfilled. On the other hand, the OR operator is written as ||, and it evaluates to true when at least one of the partial conditions is fulfilled.

You also saw a larger number of partial conditions combined into a single one. In this case, the question of operator precedence is important. With no parentheses, the AND is always evaluated before the OR. Note, however, that such conditions can become rather complex and difficult to read. It is advisable to calculate parts of the whole condition separately in advance and store them temporarily in bool-typed variables.

I also tried to bring your attention to the problem of reversing compound conditions, which requires extra care and concentration to do it right. Specifically, you learned that when reversing, the ANDs are toggled into ORs (and vice versa), and equalities change into inequalities (and vice versa).

Finally, I showed you how to check whether a number belongs either to a specified set or to a specified range. In the latter case, you perform simultaneous tests against lower and upper bounds of the range.

# CHAPTER 18

# Multiple Conditions

Staying with the topic of conditions, you will now proceed to more complex examples. In this chapter, you will meet tasks that can be solved using several conditions in a single program.

## Soccer

First, you will consider in detail a typical situation of three branches of alternative execution paths.

## Task

You will prepare a program in which the user enters data about a soccer match: the numbers of goals scored by both sides. The program then evaluates the match result. It displays whether the first club won, the second club won, or it was a tie (see Figures 18-1, 18-2, 18-3).

© Radek Vystavěl 2017
R. Vystavěl, *C# Programming for Absolute Beginners*, https://doi.org/10.1007/978-1-4842-3318-4_18

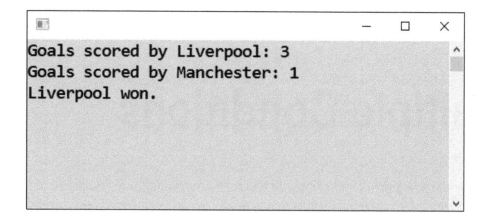

***Figure 18-1.*** *The first club won*

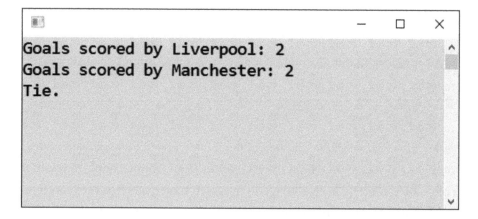

***Figure 18-2.*** *It's a tie*

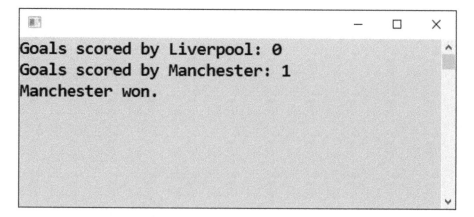

***Figure 18-3.*** *The second club won*

# Analysis

You can solve the task using three conditions in a row, each of them considering a specific match result (see Figure 18-4).

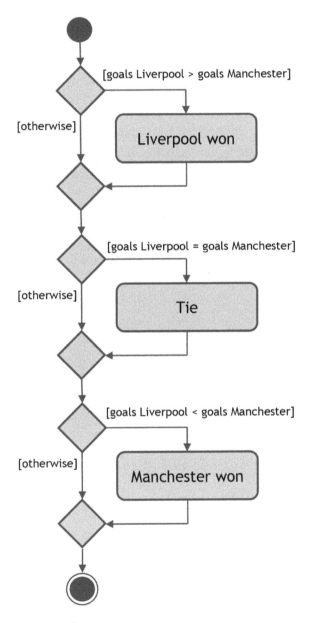

***Figure 18-4.*** *The program flow*

# Solution

Here is the code:

```
static void Main(string[] args)
{
    // Inputs
    Console.Write("Goals scored by Liverpool: ");
    string inputLiverpool = Console.ReadLine();
    int goalsLiverpool = Convert.ToInt32(inputLiverpool);

    Console.Write("Goals scored by Manchester: ");
    string inputManchester = Console.ReadLine();
    int goalsManchester = Convert.ToInt32(inputManchester);

    // Evaluating
    if (goalsLiverpool > goalsManchester)
    {
        Console.WriteLine("Liverpool won.");
    }

    if (goalsLiverpool == goalsManchester)
    {
        Console.WriteLine("Tie.");
    }

    if (goalsLiverpool < goalsManchester)
    {
        Console.WriteLine("Manchester won.");
    }

    // Waiting for Enter
    Console.ReadLine();
}
```

# Soccer Alternatively

To show you another point of view, you will solve the previous exercise in an alternative way. Previously you used three conditions in a row. This time you will nest the second condition into the first one.

## Analysis

As shown in Figure 18-5, the program will branch into the following alternatives first:

- Liverpool won.

- Liverpool did not win.

The alternative, "Liverpool did not win," will be further branched into the following:

- Tie.

- Manchester won.

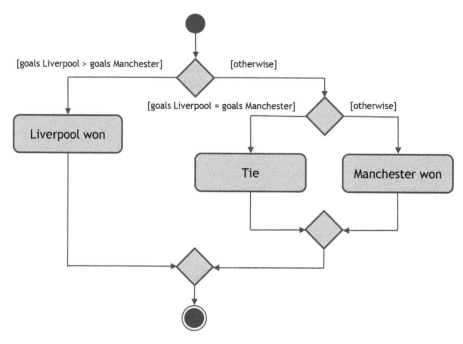

**Figure 18-5.** *The program flow*

## Solution

Here is the code:

```
static void Main(string[] args)
{
    // Inputs
    Console.Write("Goals scored by Liverpool: ");
    string inputLiverpool = Console.ReadLine();
    int goalsLiverpool = Convert.ToInt32(inputLiverpool);

    Console.Write("Goals scored by Manchester: ");
    string inputManchester = Console.ReadLine();
    int goalsManchester = Convert.ToInt32(inputManchester);
```

```
// Evaluating
if (goalsLiverpool > goalsManchester)
{
    // Here we know Liverpool won. We can display the result.
    Console.WriteLine("Liverpool won.");
}
else
{
    // Here we know Liverpool did not win. We will decide
    //   between tie and victorious Manchester
    if (goalsLiverpool == goalsManchester)
    {
        Console.WriteLine("Tie.");
    }
    else
    {
        Console.WriteLine("Manchester won.");
    }
}

// Waiting for Enter
Console.ReadLine();
}
```

# Minimum of Three Numbers

The next example uses conditional execution to compare three numbers.

# Task

You will write a program that finds the smallest of three numbers entered by the user (see Figure 18-6).

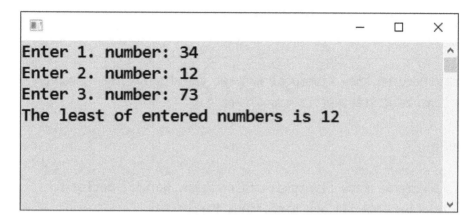

*Figure 18-6. Finding the smallest number*

## Analysis

The task can be solved by subsequent processing of all the entered numbers. You will use a helper variable to store the minimal value found so far.

At the beginning, the first entered number becomes the minimum. In the second step, you compare the second number to the minimum. If the former is less than the latter, the former becomes the minimum. Finally, the same procedure is performed with the third number.

## Solution

Here is the code:

```
static void Main(string[] args)
{
    // Inputs
    Console.Write("Enter 1. number: ");
    string input1 = Console.ReadLine();
    int number1 = Convert.ToInt32(input1);

    Console.Write("Enter 2. number: ");
    string input2 = Console.ReadLine();
    int number2 = Convert.ToInt32(input2);
```

```
Console.Write("Enter 3. number: ");
string input3 = Console.ReadLine();
int number3 = Convert.ToInt32(input3);

// At the beginning, we set 1st number as minimum
int minimum = number1;

// Is not 2nd number less than present minimum?
if (number2 < minimum)
{
    minimum = number2;
}

// Is not 3rd number less than present minimum?
if (number3 < minimum)
{
    minimum = number3;
}

// Output
Console.WriteLine("The least of entered numbers is " + minimum);

// Waiting for Enter
Console.ReadLine();
}
```

# Minimum with Built-in Function

You can solve the previous exercise using the Math.Min function, which is readily available in C#. The function itself determines the least of two numbers. I will show you how to use it for the case of three numbers.

## Solution

First you determine the smallest of the first and second numbers. The result will then "compete" with the third one.

Here is the code:

```
static void Main(string[] args)
{
    // Inputs
    Console.Write("Enter 1. number: ");
    string input1 = Console.ReadLine();
    int number1 = Convert.ToInt32(input1);

    Console.Write("Enter 2. number: ");
    string input2 = Console.ReadLine();
    int number2 = Convert.ToInt32(input2);

    Console.Write("Enter 3. number: ");
    string input3 = Console.ReadLine();
    int number3 = Convert.ToInt32(input3);

    // Evaluating
    int min12 = Math.Min(number1, number2);
    int minimum = Math.Min(min12, number3);

    // Output
    Console.WriteLine("The least of entered numbers is " + minimum);

    // Waiting for Enter
    Console.ReadLine();
}
```

# Linear Equation

This exercise will get a bit into mathematics.

# Task

You will write a program to solve a linear equation, in other words, an equation of the type $ax + b = 0$.

For example, $2x + 6 = 0$ is a linear equation, with the 2 being $a$ and the 6 being $b$.

The solution is clearly -3. When you substitute -3 for $x$, the left side becomes zero, in other words, equal to the right side.

The user enters the equation to be solved in the form of the coefficients $a$ and $b$. The program then calculates and displays its solution (see Figure 18-7).

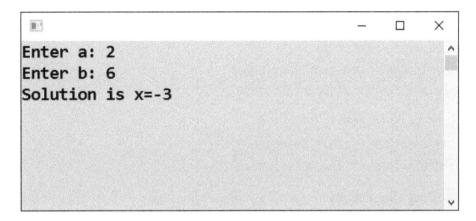

**Figure 18-7.** *Calculating and displaying its solution*

# Analysis

Whenever you want to program anything, you need to understand the real-world problem first. In other words, you need to know how to solve it without a computer.

What follows is a mathematical reminder of how to solve a linear equation:

- If $a$ is not zero, the obvious solution is $-b/a$.

- The case of $a$ equal to zero is a kind of mathematical curiosity. The equation degenerates to a strange "equation without $x$" or the pseudo-equation $b = 0$. Such an "equation"

  - Has infinitely many solutions for $b$ equal to zero (it always holds regardless of $x$)

  - Does not have a solution for a nonzero $b$ (no $x$ can fulfill the equation)

257

# Solution

Here is the code:

```csharp
static void Main(string[] args)
{
    // Inputs
    Console.Write("Enter a: ");
    string inputA = Console.ReadLine();
    double a = Convert.ToDouble(inputA);

    Console.Write("Enter b: ");
    string inputB = Console.ReadLine();
    double b = Convert.ToDouble(inputB);

    // Solving the equation
    if (a != 0)
    {
        // a is non-zero, the equation has "normal" solution
        double solution = -b / a;
        Console.WriteLine("Solution is x=" + solution);
    }
    else
    {
        // a is zero, result depends on b
        if (b == 0)
        {
            Console.WriteLine("The equation \"is solved\" by any x");
        }
        else
        {
            Console.WriteLine("The equation does not have a solution");
        }
    }

    // Waiting for Enter
    Console.ReadLine();
}
```

# Quadratic Equation

Staying with mathematics, the next exercise concerns a more difficult quadratic equation.

## Task

You will write a program to solve a quadratic equation, in other words, an equation like $ax^2 + bx + c = 0$. An example of a quadratic equation is $x^2 - x - 2 = 0$ with $a$ being 1, $b$ being -1, and $c$ being -2. The equation mentioned has two solutions: -1 and 2. Substituting any of the two zeros the left side.

The equation to be solved will be entered in the form of the coefficients $a$, $b$, and $c$. The program calculates and displays its solution (see Figure 18-8).

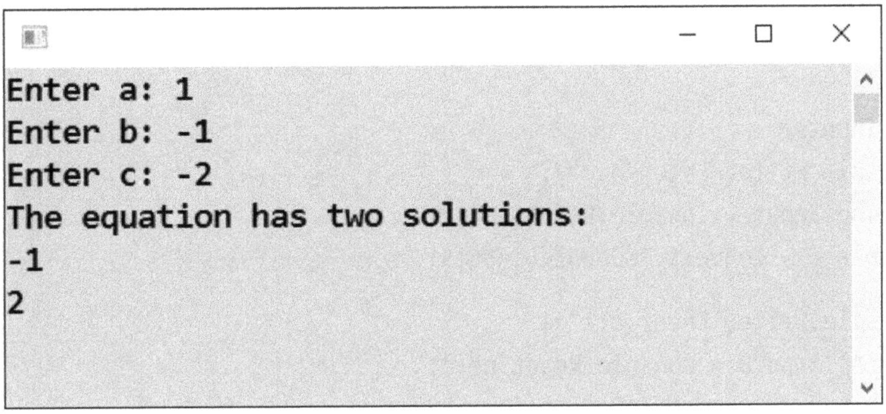

*Figure 18-8.* *Solving a quadratic equation*

For the sake of simplicity, you will not consider the case of $a$ equal to zero, which would transfer the task to the previous one, a linear equation.

## Analysis

Once upon a time, someone clever worked out a procedure to solve quadratic equations. You probably know it from school. You calculate the so-called discriminant first.

$$D = b^2 - 4ac$$

The solution then branches according to the discriminant value.

- For $D > 0$, the equation has two solutions given by the following:

$$x_{1,2} = \frac{-b \pm \sqrt{D}}{2a}$$

- For $D = 0$, the same formula applies with the two solutions coinciding.

- For $D < 0$, the equation does not have a solution in real numbers.

## Solution

Here is the code:

```
static void Main(string[] args)
{
    // Inputs
    Console.Write("Enter a: ");
    string input = Console.ReadLine();
    double a = Convert.ToDouble(input);

    Console.Write("Enter b: ");
    string inputB = Console.ReadLine();
    double b = Convert.ToDouble(inputB);

    Console.Write("Enter c: ");
    string inputC = Console.ReadLine();
    double c = Convert.ToDouble(inputC);

    // Solving + output
    double d = b * b - 4 * a * c;
    if (d > 0)
    {
        double x1 = (-b - Math.Sqrt(d)) / (2 * a);
        double x2 = (-b + Math.Sqrt(d)) / (2 * a);
```

```
        Console.WriteLine("The equation has two solutions:");
        Console.WriteLine(x1);
        Console.WriteLine(x2);
    }
    if (d == 0)
    {
        double x = -b / (2 * a);
        Console.WriteLine("The equation has a single solution: " + x);
    }
    if (d < 0)
    {
        Console.WriteLine("The equation does not have a solution");
    }

    // Waiting for Enter
    Console.ReadLine();
}
```

## Discussion

The most interesting point of this exercise is the way you enter the formula in code. Note that the numerator and the denominator have to be enclosed in parentheses to ascertain the correct order of calculations! The mathematical formula does not contain them because mathematicians use fractions.

When calculating the discriminant, I do not use parentheses; I just rely on the precedence of multiplication to subtraction.

## Test

To check that the program calculates correctly, you can write further code as a test; the left side should become zero after substituting the solution for *x*.

# Summary

In this chapter, you saw several examples of using more than one condition to do the task assigned.

First, you solved a soccer match evaluation in two alternative ways. The first one considered the individual possibilities one after another using three simple `if` statements. The second one used a branch nested inside another branch.

You further exercised multiple conditions in a row one after another to find the smallest of three numbers. To do this, you stored a "minimum-so-far" value in a helper variable.

The same task was then solved using the built-in function `Math.Min`. You already know that the function determines the minimum of two values. Here I showed you an interesting case of how you can use it for three numbers.

In the final two tasks, you practiced multiple conditions in examples from mathematics, namely, solving linear and quadratic equations. The last task gave you the opportunity to see a bit more complex calculation written in code.

# CHAPTER 19

# Advanced Conditions

The third part of this book concludes with several tasks concerning conditional execution that may be considered advanced. First you will study the conditional operator, then you will write a program containing several complex conditions, and finally you will learn about an important maxim: when you want to test something, you must be sure it exists.

## Conditional Operator

In many cases, the if-else construction can be replaced with the conditional operator, which results in one of the two values depending on whether a condition is or is not fulfilled. If you know the IF function of Excel, you will find the conditional operator familiar.

## Task

You will solve the former "Head and Tail" task (from Chapter 16) using the conditional operator (see Figure 19-1).

*Figure 19-1.* *Using the conditional operator*

© Radek Vystavěl 2017
R. Vystavěl, *C# Programming for Absolute Beginners*, https://doi.org/10.1007/978-1-4842-3318-4_19

# Solution

Here's the code:

```
static void Main(string[] args)
{
    // Random number generator
    Random randomNumbers = new Random();

    // Random number 0/1 and its transformation
    int randomNumber = randomNumbers.Next(0, 1 + 1);
    string message = randomNumber == 0 ? "Head tossed" : "Tail tossed";
    Console.WriteLine(message);

    // Waiting for Enter
    Console.ReadLine();
}
```

# Discussion

The conditional operator (?:) syntax looks like this:

```
        condition ? yesValue : noValue
```

The result of such an expression is as follows:

- *yesValue* if the *condition* holds (is fulfilled)

- *noValue* otherwise

## The Program

In this case, the condition is an equality test of the randomNumber variable against zero. If it is true, the message variable is assigned the "Head tossed" text. Otherwise, it is assigned the "Tail tossed" text.

## Terminology

The conditional operator is also called a *ternary* operator since it is the only operator that accepts three operands (values it works with): a condition, a *yesValue*, and a *noValue*.

# Summary Evaluation

Now you will exercise more complex conditions in a realistic situation.

## Task

The task is to write a program for summary evaluation of a student (see Figure 19-2). The user enters grades from four subjects (in the range 1 to 5, with 1 being the best). The user also specifies whether the student being considered had some unexcused absences or not. The program then gives a summary evaluation, which is a kind of overall score.

- Excellent

- Good

- Failed

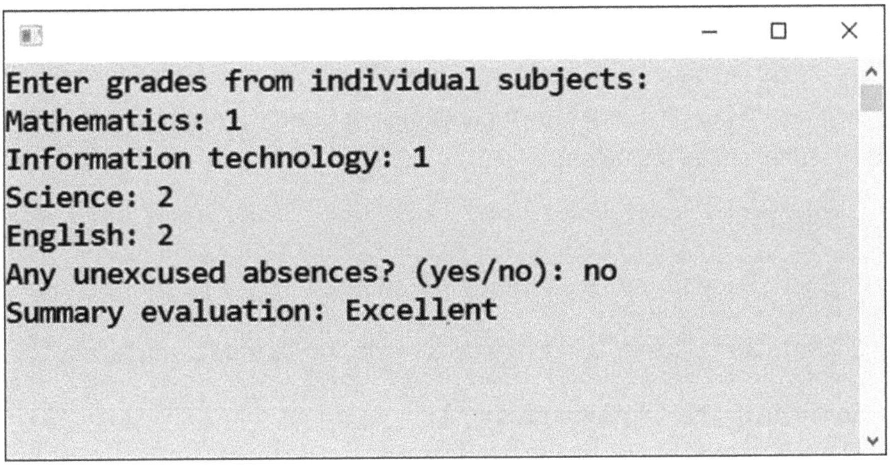

*Figure 19-2.* *Summary evaluation of a student*

## Details

I emphasized in Chapter 18 that to be able to program anything, you need to exactly understand the task being solved. In the current exercise, you need to specify the exact criteria for summary evaluation.

A student has an *Excellent* evaluation when

- The arithmetic average of all the grades is not higher than 1.5

- The student does not have any grade worse than 2

- The student does not have any unexcused absences

The student is considered *Failed* when at least one of her grades is 5.
In all other cases, the summary evaluation is *Good*.
You can probably guess now that the program is not going to be trivial.

# Solution

Here's the code:

```
static void Main(string[] args)
{
    // 1. PREPARATIONS
    string errorMessage = "Incorrect input";
    int mathematics, informationTechnology, science, english;
    bool hasUnexcusedAbsences;

    // 2. INPUTS
    try
    {
        Console.WriteLine("Enter grades from individual subjects:");

        Console.Write("Mathematics: ");
        string input = Console.ReadLine();
        mathematics = Convert.ToInt32(input);
        if (mathematics < 1 || mathematics > 5)
        {
            Console.WriteLine(errorMessage);
            return;
        }

        Console.Write("Information technology: ");
        input = Console.ReadLine();
        informationTechnology = Convert.ToInt32(input);
```

```
    if (informationTechnology < 1 || informationTechnology > 5)
    {
        Console.WriteLine(errorMessage);
        return;
    }

    Console.Write("Science: ");
    input = Console.ReadLine();
    science = Convert.ToInt32(input);
    if (science < 1 || science > 5)
    {
        Console.WriteLine(errorMessage);
        return;
    }

    Console.Write("English: ");
    input = Console.ReadLine();
    english = Convert.ToInt32(input);
    if (english < 1 || english > 5)
    {
        Console.WriteLine(errorMessage);
        return;
    }

    Console.Write("Any unexcused absences? (yes/no): ");
    input = Console.ReadLine();
    input = input.ToLower(); // not distinguishing upper/lower
    if (input != "yes" && input != "no")
    {
        Console.WriteLine(errorMessage);
        return;
    }
    hasUnexcusedAbsences = input == "yes";
}
catch (Exception)
{
    Console.WriteLine(errorMessage);
```

```
        return;
    }

    // 3. EVALUATION
    // You need arithmetic average of all the grades
    double average = (mathematics + informationTechnology + science +
    english) / 4.0;
    string message;

    // Testing all conditions for excellence
    if (average < 1.5001 &&
        mathematics <= 2 && informationTechnology <= 2 &&
        science <= 2 && english <= 2 &&
        !hasUnexcusedAbsences)
    {
        message = "Excellent";
    }
    else
    {
        // Here you know the result is not excellent, so testing the other
        two possibilities
        if (mathematics == 5 || informationTechnology == 5 ||
            science == 5 || english == 5)
        {
            message = "Failed";
        }
        else
        {
            message = "Good";
        }
    }

    // 4. OUTPUT
    Console.WriteLine("Summary evaluation: " + message);

    // Waiting for Enter
    Console.ReadLine();
}
```

# Discussion

The following sections explain the program.

## Grade Inputs

In this exercise, you thoroughly care about doing an input data check. A `try-catch` wraps the whole input section. You also need to check whether the grades belong in the 1 to 5 range.

Note that a grade less than 1 or greater than 5 signalizes an error. You use the || operator ("at least one").

## Program Termination

An erroneous input terminates the program immediately. You use the `return` statement here that terminates a subprogram in general. However, when used inside `Main`, it directly terminates the whole program.

## Yes/No Input

To enter whether the student had some unexcused absences, the user enters either yes or no. The input difference from both yes and no signalizes an error. I use && operator ("at the same time").

Before the check, you convert the input into lowercase so that it does not mind when the user uses capital letters.

What is interesting is the line containing both single and double equal signs (single for assignment, double for comparison):

```
hasUnexcusedAbsences = input == "yes";
```

The "work" of the == operator results in either a `true` or `false` value according to whether the equality holds. The resulting value is then assigned into the `bool`-typed `hasUnexcusedAbsences` variable.

## Beware of Integer Division!

When calculating the grade average, you divide the sum by the value of 4.0, not by the value of 4. You do not want the computer to consider the slash as an integer division operator. That is why you are avoiding the division of `int` by `int`.

If you entered just 4, then the case of 1, 2, 2, 2 grades would be mistakenly evaluated as Excellent since the average would be calculated to a precise 1 instead of the correct 1.75!

## Decimal Arithmetic

Why did you enter the check of the average as follows?

```
average < 1.5001
```

Why didn't you use the following?

```
average <= 1.5
```

?

It was because decimal arithmetic does not have to be precise. Sometimes it is possible that the computer calculates something like 1.500000000001 instead of the correct 1.5. That is why you use a little bit greater number in the test.

# Second Character Test

Many programs crash because a programmer forgot to test that something exists before accessing it. This task will be your first acquaintance with this frequent issue.

## Task

I will show you how to test the second character of the entered text. Let's say a product label has to always have a capital X in the second position (see Figure 19-3 and Figure 19-4).

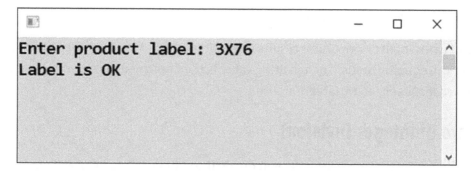

*Figure 19-3.* *Testing the second character, correct*

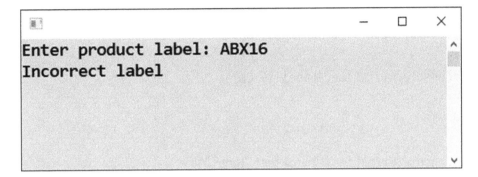

*Figure 19-4.* *Testing the second character, incorrect*

Why is such a test so important that I have decided to get you acquainted with it? You need to test first whether the second character exists at all. This is what you will often meet; you will not be able to test something until you have found that something exists!

In this case, the program must not crash upon empty or too short input (see Figure 19-5).

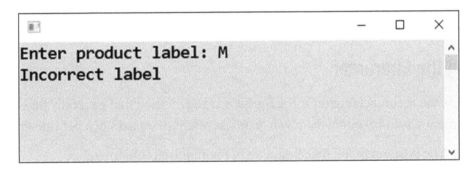

*Figure 19-5.* *Incorrect label, not crashing*

## Solution

Here's the code:

```
static void Main(string[] args)
{
    // Input
    Console.Write("Enter product label: ");
    string label = Console.ReadLine();
```

```
    // Evaluating
    if (label.Length >= 2 && label.Substring(1, 1) == "X")
    {
        Console.WriteLine("Label is OK");
    }
    else
    {
        Console.WriteLine("Incorrect label");
    }

    // Waiting for Enter
    Console.ReadLine();
}
```

# Discussion

The following sections explain the program.

## Getting the Character

You access the second character using the Substring method that generally pulls a specific part (*substring*) out of the given text. The method requires two parameters.

- The position of the first character of the required substring. The position numbering starts with zero, so the second character position is 1.

- The number of characters of the required substring. In this case, what you need is just a single character, which is why the second parameter is 1, too.

## Existence Test

The test of whether a given character equals something has a hidden catch: the second character does not have to exist at all. This happens when the user enters zero or one character.

In such a case, the Substring(1,1) call would cause a runtime error.

This means you have to test first whether the text is at least two characters long. Only if this test passes can you access the second character.

There is a compound condition in the code, as shown here:

```
if (label.Length >= 2 && label.Substring(1, 1) == "X")
```

Its functioning relies upon the *short-circuit evaluation* of the && operator. If the first partial condition of an AND join does not hold, the second one is not evaluated at all, since it is useless. Even if it held, it would not change the overall result because the AND operator requires both parts to hold simultaneously.

In this case, when the length of a label is less than 2, then the Substring call, which would fail, is skipped, and the program does not crash!

Note that an analogous statement can be made about the || operator, too.

## An Experiment

Try to omit the first partial condition (the length check). Then enter a single character as a user. The program would terminate with a runtime error. This way you will see that the first condition really is important.

# Summary

In this chapter, you studied several examples of advanced conditions.

You started with the so-called conditional operator (?:), which is also called a ternary operator because it works with three values. Depending on fulfillment of the specified condition (the first value, before the question mark), the operator's "work" results in either *yesValue* (the second value, between the question mark and the colon) or *noValue* (the third value, after the colon). The conditional operator is a suitable shortcut replacement for certain types of if-else situations.

The middle task of summary evaluation was a kind of recap of all the things you learned about conditional execution. There you have met various tests and many compound conditions, as well as negation with the ! operator.

The final task of testing the second character of some text has shown you the importance of testing that the second character exists at all before you explore what it is. There you used the short-circuit evaluation of conditions. If the result of a compound condition can be decided already after the first partial condition is evaluated, then the second partial condition is skipped altogether.

# PART IV

# Loops

# CHAPTER 20

# First Loops

You are entering the most difficult chapters of this book. Loops are a mighty tool that all programmers need as much as the air they breathe. Understanding loops is not simple, which is why you will go through many exercises with loops.

## Repeating the Same Text

A loop is a tool to efficiently write repetitions of the same or more often a similar activity. So that you can properly appreciate loops, you will solve some of the tasks twice, first without a loop and then with it. You will start with some repetition of the same activity, and after that you will move on to using loops to repeat similar activities.

## Task

You will write a program that displays "I will start learning tomorrow." ten times in a row (see Figure 20-1).

© Radek Vystavěl 2017
R. Vystavěl, *C# Programming for Absolute Beginners*, https://doi.org/10.1007/978-1-4842-3318-4_20

```
I will start learning tomorrow.
I will start learning tomorrow.
I will start learning tomorrow.
I will start learning tomorrow.
I will start learning tomorrow.
I will start learning tomorrow.
I will start learning tomorrow.
I will start learning tomorrow.
I will start learning tomorrow.
I will start learning tomorrow.
```

*Figure 20-1.* *Ten repetitions*

## Solution

Here is the code:

```
static void Main(string[] args)
{
    // Output
    Console.WriteLine("I will start learning tomorrow.");
    Console.WriteLine("I will start learning tomorrow.");
    Console.WriteLine("I will start learning tomorrow.");
    Console.WriteLine("I will start learning tomorrow.");
    Console.WriteLine("I will start learning tomorrow.");

    Console.WriteLine("I will start learning tomorrow.");
    Console.WriteLine("I will start learning tomorrow.");
    Console.WriteLine("I will start learning tomorrow.");
    Console.WriteLine("I will start learning tomorrow.");
    Console.WriteLine("I will start learning tomorrow.");

    // Waiting for Enter
    Console.ReadLine();
}
```

## Solution Using a Loop

Think a bit about the previous exercise. Can you imagine that someone might want you to change the displayed sentence? Can you imagine repeating it a hundred times rather than ten times? Can you imagine the number of repetitions being entered by the user?

To solve these problems, you need a new tool: a loop.

## Solution

Here is the code:

```
static void Main(string[] args)
{
    // Output
    for (int count = 0; count < 10; count++)
    {
        Console.WriteLine("I will start learning tomorrow.");
    }

    // Waiting for Enter
    Console.ReadLine();
}
```

## How the for Loop Works

You use the for construction to indicate repetition. Its general syntax looks like this:

```
for (initializer; loopCondition; iterator)
{
    statement;
    statement;
    statement;
    ...
}
```

The for loop works like this:

- initializer is performed once before entering the loop.

- loopCondition is being evaluated before every turn of the loop. If it holds, the computer enters the loop and executes the statements inside its body.

- The iterator statement is executed after every turn of the loop is completed. After that, loopCondition is evaluated again.

Figure 20-2 shows the program flow.

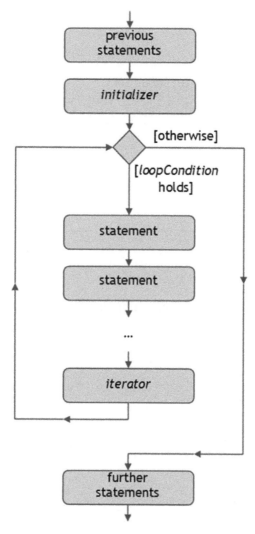

**Figure 20-2.**  *The program flow*

# The Loop

In this case, the required number of repetitions is achieved by counting the loop turns performed so far. For that purpose, you use the count variable.

At the beginning (*initializer*), the variable is set to zero.

After completing every loop turn (*iterator*), the variable is incremented by one.

The loop body (the display of a line of text) is repeated as long as (loopCondition) the number of lines in the output has not reached ten. As soon as the count variable becomes 10, the condition (count < 10 or 10 < 10) will no longer be fulfilled, the loop will terminate, and the computer will continue executing the statements following the loop.

# Explore It Yourself

You should take the time to explore the inner workings of loops to grasp them thoroughly. Use debugging tools you already know: stepping and inspecting the count variable.

# Tip

Visual Studio can help you write a for loop without mistakes. Just enter for, press the Tab key twice, and edit the generated loop header.

# Choosing the Number of Repetitions

The for loop allows you to solve cases when you do not know the number of repetitions in advance (at the time of code writing).

# Task

You will modify the previous exercise to let the user specify the number of the sentence repetitions (see Figure 20-3).

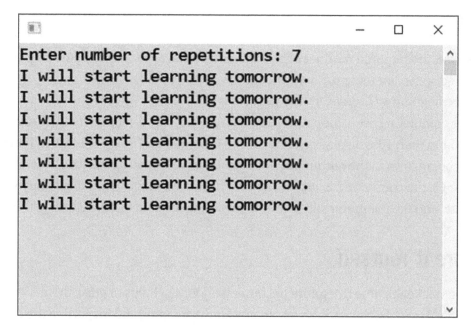

*Figure 20-3.* *Letting the user specify the number of sentence repetitions*

## Solution

Here's the code:

```
static void Main(string[] args)
{
    // Input
    Console.Write("Enter number of repetitions: ");
    string input = Console.ReadLine();
    int howManyTimes = Convert.ToInt32(input);

    // Output
    for (int count = 0; count < howManyTimes; count++)
    {
        Console.WriteLine("I will start learning tomorrow.");
    }

    // Waiting for Enter
    Console.ReadLine();
}
```

## Discussion

Note the following:

- Compared to the previous task, you replaced the fixed number of repetitions with a variable value entered by the user.

- Carefully choose the name of the variable to store the required total number of repetitions; here it's howManyTimes. Specifically, you should distinguish it from the count variable storing the current number of repetitions.

## Throwing a Die Repeatedly

You will see one more example of repeating the same activity.

## Task

You will write a program that throws a die 20 times (see Figure 20-4).

**Figure 20-4.** *Throwing a die 20 times*

## Solution

Here's the code:

```
static void Main(string[] args)
{
    // Random number generator
    Random randomNumbers = new Random();
```

```
// Output
for (int count = 0; count < 20; count++)
{
    int thrown = randomNumbers.Next(1, 6 + 1);
    Console.Write(thrown.ToString() + " ");
}

// Waiting for Enter
Console.ReadLine();
}
```

# Repeating Similar Lines

What if the repeated activity was not the same but just similar?

## Task

You will output ten similar lines, differing only in the printed line number (see Figure 20-5).

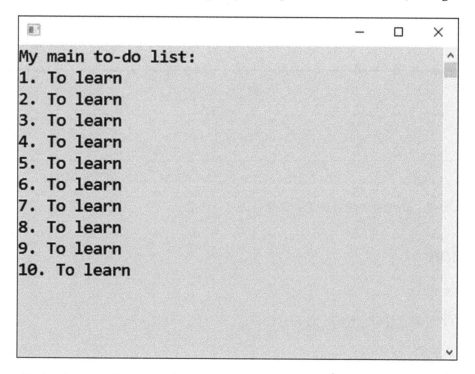

***Figure 20-5.*** *Outputting something similar ten times*

## Solution Without a Loop

Again, you can start with a solution without a loop to appreciate the importance of loops.

Here's the code:

```
static void Main(string[] args)
{
    // Output
    Console.WriteLine("My main to-do list:");

    Console.WriteLine("1. To learn");
    Console.WriteLine("2. To learn");
    Console.WriteLine("3. To learn");
    Console.WriteLine("4. To learn");
    Console.WriteLine("5. To learn");
    Console.WriteLine("6. To learn");
    Console.WriteLine("7. To learn");
    Console.WriteLine("8. To learn");
    Console.WriteLine("9. To learn");
    Console.WriteLine("10. To learn");

    // Waiting for Enter
    Console.ReadLine();
}
```

## Solution Using a Loop

Loops can efficiently solve this type of problem. Actually, you will find yourself incorporating loops to repeat similar activities more often than to repeat precisely the same ones.

```
static void Main(string[] args)
{
    // Output
    Console.WriteLine("My main to-do list:");

    for (int taskNumber = 1; taskNumber <= 10; taskNumber++)
    {
```

```
        Console.WriteLine(taskNumber.ToString() + ". To learn");
    }

    // Waiting for Enter
    Console.ReadLine();
}
```

## Discussion

The following sections discuss the program.

### Control Variable

The core of the solution is to use the value of the loop's control variable inside its body. In this program, you name the variable `taskNumber`, and you use its value for output.

This is how you achieve displaying 1 in the first passage of the loop, 2 in the second passage, and so on.

Check the situation yourself using your debugging tools.

### The Loop Starts at 1

The previous exercise (repeatedly throwing a die) used the loop with its control variable running from 0 to 19. Contrary to that, this time it was more convenient to start at 1 rather than at 0. This change also caused the loop condition to change. You used a "less than or equal" test rather than a "less than" one.

## Summary

The chapter introduced you to the topic of loops, which are a mighty programming tool allowing you to specify repetitions of the same or, more often, a similar activity.

For loops, C# offers several programming constructs; you learned about the most fundamental `for` loop in this chapter. In the code, the `for` loop consists of a header controlling the loop and a body consisting of the statements to be repeated surrounded with braces. The header itself consists of three parts separated by semicolons,

- The *initializer* is the statement to be executed once before the loop starts "revolving."

- The *loop condition* is the condition evaluated before each turn of the loop. If it is fulfilled (i.e., evaluated to `true`), another round of statements of the loop's body is executed. If it is not fulfilled (i.e., evaluated to `false`), the loop is terminated, and the program's execution continues to the statements after the loop.

- The *iterator* is the statement to be executed after each turn of the loop.

To get a deeper understanding of how `for` loops work, definitely use debugging tools like stepping and memory inspection.

The `for` loop is most often controlled by a variable working more or less like a counter of loop turns. This variable is called the *control variable*. In the last task, you learned how to use the value of the control variable also inside the loop's body.

# CHAPTER 21

# Improving Loops

As you've learned, loops are mighty, and they are not trivial. That is why all the remaining chapters of the book are dedicated to understanding loops better. Let's proceed to some more difficult exercises.

## Choosing Text

First, you will return to the exercise with text repetition from the previous chapter and improve on it.

## Task

In the section "Choosing the Number of Repetitions," the user was allowed to vary the number of repetitions of a given sentence. Now you will allow the user to vary the sentence itself (see Figure 21-1).

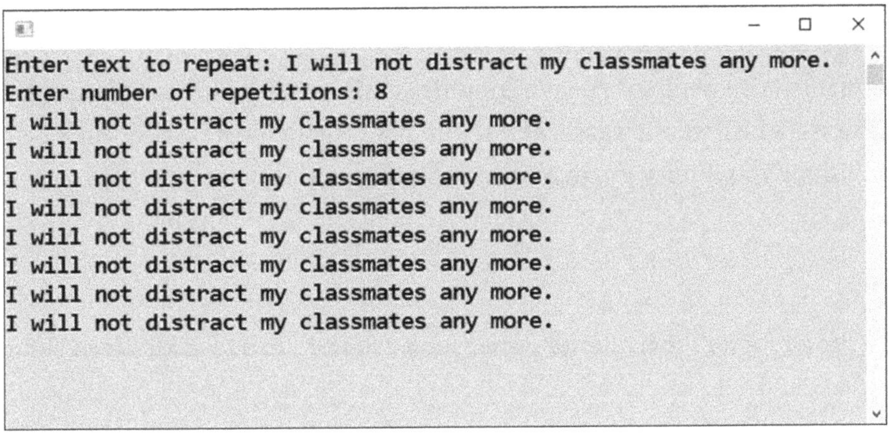

*Figure 21-1. Varying a sentence*

© Radek Vystavěl 2017
R. Vystavěl, *C# Programming for Absolute Beginners*, https://doi.org/10.1007/978-1-4842-3318-4_21

## Solution

Here's the code:

```
static void Main(string[] args)
{
    // Inputs
    Console.Write("Enter text to repeat: ");
    string textToRepeat = Console.ReadLine();

    Console.Write("Enter number of repetitions: ");
    string input = Console.ReadLine();
    int howManyTimes = Convert.ToInt32(input);

    // Output
    for (int count = 0; count < howManyTimes; count++)
    {
        Console.WriteLine(textToRepeat);
    }

    // Waiting for Enter
    Console.ReadLine();
}
```

## Alternating Loop

Quite frequently, you need to repeat a couple of activities. You do the first thing, then the second one, and the first one again, and so on. It is interesting to look at such a task in code. I will show you three ways of how to solve this.

## Task

You will write a program that alternates between two tasks in a to-do list (see Figure 21-2).

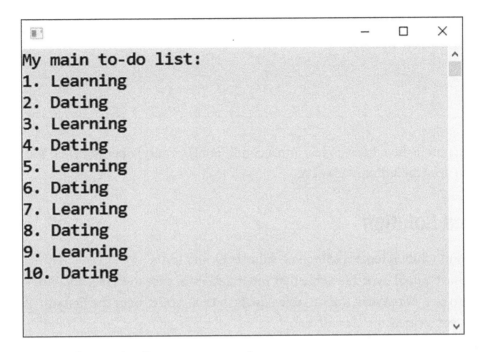

*Figure 21-2.* *Alternating between two tasks*

# First Solution

The first solution is based on distinguishing whether the loop's control variable, which is running from 1 to 10, is odd or even. When it is odd, you display "Learning." When it is even, you display "Dating."

An odd/even test will be performed by checking the remainder after integer division by 2. Just to remind you, the remainder is calculated using the percent sign (%) operator in C#.

```
static void Main(string[] args)
{
    // Output
    Console.WriteLine("My main to-do list:");

    for (int taskNumber = 1; taskNumber <= 10; taskNumber++)
    {
        string taskText = taskNumber % 2 != 0 ? "Learning" : "Dating";
        Console.WriteLine(taskNumber.ToString() + ". " + taskText);
    }
```

```
    // Waiting for Enter
    Console.ReadLine();
}
```

## Note

You incorporate the odd/even test into a conditional (ternary) operator (`?:`). You could have also used an ordinary `if-else`.

## Second Solution

The second solution toggles a Boolean value back and forth.

You have a `bool`-typed variable that you toggle from `true` to `false`, and vice versa, in every turn of a loop. When the variable equals to `true`, you display the first text. When it is `false`, you display the second one.

```
static void Main(string[] args)
{
    // Preparations
    Console.WriteLine("My main to-do list:");
    bool learning = true;

    for (int taskNumber = 1; taskNumber <= 10; taskNumber++)
    {
        // Output
        string taskText = learning ? "Learning" : "Dating";
        Console.WriteLine(taskNumber.ToString() + ". " + taskText);

        // Toggling of the flag
        learning = !learning;
    }

    // Waiting for Enter
    Console.ReadLine();
}
```

## Notes

Note the following:

- The condition does not have to be entered as `learning == true`. The `learning` variable is already `bool`-typed, which means you can use it directly as a condition. When it is `true`, the condition holds.

- You need to set the initial value of the variable before entering the loop. The initial value is used during the first turn of the loop. In this case, you set it to `true`.

- Toggling from `true` to `false`, and vice versa, is performed using the negation operator (`!`).

## Third Solution

The third approach to the solution is to repeat the loop five times rather than ten times and to perform both "odd activity" and "even activity" in a single turn of the loop.

Here's the code:

```
static void Main(string[] args)
{
    // Preparations
    Console.WriteLine("My main to-do list:");
    int taskNumber = 1;

    for (int coupleCount = 0; coupleCount < 5; coupleCount++)
    {
        // Couple output and adjusting task number
        Console.WriteLine(taskNumber.ToString() + ". Learning");
        taskNumber++;
        Console.WriteLine(taskNumber.ToString() + ". Dating");
        taskNumber++;
    }

    // Waiting for Enter
    Console.ReadLine();
}
```

# Rock-Scissors-Paper

In the next exercise, you will see the for loop with many statements inside its body. The looping will represent individual rounds of a game.

## Task

You will write a program that plays a specified number of rounds of the rock-scissors-paper game with the user (see Figure 21-3).

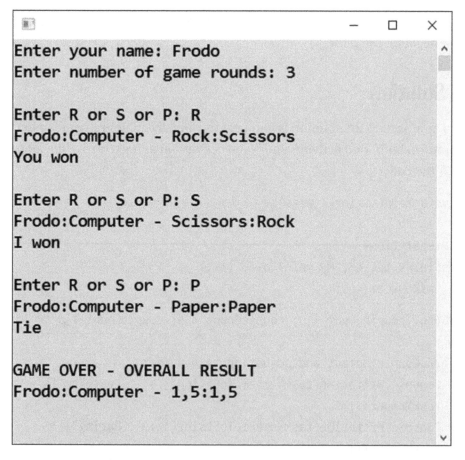

**Figure 21-3.** *The game*

Scoring will be similar to chess: one point for a victory and half a point for a tie.

# Solution

Here's the code:

```
static void Main(string[] args)
{
    // Preparations
    Random randomNumbers = new Random();

    double playerPoints = 0;
    double computerPoints = 0;

    int rock = 1, scissors = 2, paper = 3;

    // Inputs
    Console.Write("Enter your name: ");
    string playerName = Console.ReadLine();

    Console.Write("Enter number of game rounds: ");
    string input = Console.ReadLine();
    int totalRounds = Convert.ToInt32(input);

    Console.WriteLine();

    // Individual rounds
    for (int roundNumber = 0; roundNumber < totalRounds; roundNumber++)
    {
        // Computer chooses
        int computerChoice = randomNumbers.Next(1, 3 + 1);

        // Player chooses
        Console.Write("Enter R or S or P: ");
        string playerInput = Console.ReadLine();
        string playerInputUppercase = playerInput.ToUpper();
        int playerChoice = playerInputUppercase == "R" ?
            rock : (playerInputUppercase == "S" ? scissors : paper);

        // Round evaluation
        string message = "";
        if (computerChoice == rock && playerChoice == scissors ||
```

```
                computerChoice == scissors && playerChoice == paper ||
                computerChoice == paper && playerChoice == rock)
        {
            // Computer won
            computerPoints += 1;
            message = "I won";
        }
        else
        {
            // Tie or player won
            if (computerChoice == playerChoice)
            {
                // Tie
                computerPoints += 0.5;
                playerPoints += 0.5;
                message = "Tie";
            }
            else
            {
                // Player won
                playerPoints += 1;
                message = "You won";
            }
        }

    // Round output
    string playerChoiceInText = playerChoice == rock ?
        "Rock" : (playerChoice == scissors ? "Scissors" : "Paper");
    string computerChoiceInText = computerChoice == rock ?
        "Rock" : (computerChoice == scissors ? "Scissors" : "Paper");
    Console.WriteLine(playerName + ":Computer - " +
        playerChoiceInText + ":" + computerChoiceInText);
    Console.WriteLine(message);
    Console.WriteLine();
} // End of loop for game round
```

```
    // Game evaluation
    Console.WriteLine("GAME OVER - OVERALL RESULT");
    Console.WriteLine(playerName + ":Computer - " +
        playerPoints.ToString() + ":" + computerPoints.ToString());

    // Waiting for Enter
    Console.ReadLine();
}
```

## Discussion

Note the following:

- The computer "chooses" using random numbers: 1 for rock, 2 for scissors, and 3 for paper.

- For the sake of simplicity, when the user enters something other than R, S, or P, you take it as "paper."

- You do not distinguish between lowercase and uppercase in user input.

- In several places, threefold branching is solved using two nested conditional (ternary) operators rather than using two nested if-elses. Note carefully how noValue of the first conditional operator is specified using another conditional operator, which is enclosed in parentheses.

- If you do not like the conditional (ternary) operator, simply do not use it. It is just a shortcut of a special if-else case. I personally like it very much, so I use it frequently.

## Summary

In this chapter, you continued your study of the loops. The first exercise was basically a reminder of what you learned in the previous chapter. You modified one of the previous tasks.

Next you were exposed to several ways of solving alternating loops, i.e., loops repeating similar pairs of activities. Specifically, you studied the following solutions:

- Alternating output based on whether the control variable is odd or even

- Toggling a `bool` variable indicating whether you want the first output or not

- Performing both activities of the pair in a single turn of the loop

The final example of the rock-scissors-paper game was actually not centered on looping. The loop was just the means to repeat the game rounds. One game round was an example of a real, more complex procedure that you could make with what you have learned in this book so far.

# CHAPTER 22

# Number Series

Several programming tasks reduce to generating regular number series. This is what you are going to study in this chapter. You will also get a better understanding of loops this way.

## Every Other

You are already able to generate a simple number series, say from one to ten. You will tackle generating a bit more complex series now.

## Task

In this task, you will display "every other" number until 20 (see Figure 22-1).

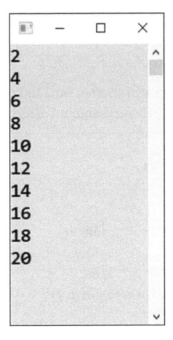

***Figure 22-1.*** *Displaying every other number*

© Radek Vystavěl 2017

R. Vystavěl, *C# Programming for Absolute Beginners*, https://doi.org/10.1007/978-1-4842-3318-4_22

# Solution

Here's the code:

```
static void Main(string[] args)
{
    // Output
    for (int number = 2; number <= 20; number += 2)
    {
        Console.WriteLine(number);
    }

    // Waiting for Enter
    Console.ReadLine();
}
```

# Discussion

The most difficult point of the exercise is to realize how to write an *iterator* of the for loop. Since you want to augment the number variable by 2, the corresponding statement will be number += 2.

# Alternative Solution

It is interesting to solve the exercise in another way. You can have an ordinary loop from 1 to 10 stepping by 1 and display twice the amount of its control variable rather than the variable itself.

```
static void Main(string[] args)
{
    // Output
    for (int line = 1; line <= 10; line++)
    {
        int displayedNumber = 2 * line;
        Console.WriteLine(displayedNumber);
    }
```

```
    // Waiting for Enter
    Console.ReadLine();
}
```

# Descending Series

What if the numbers in the series were descending? Many things will change then. Let's take a look.

## Task

In this task, you will display numbers going down from 10 to 1 (see Figure 22-2).

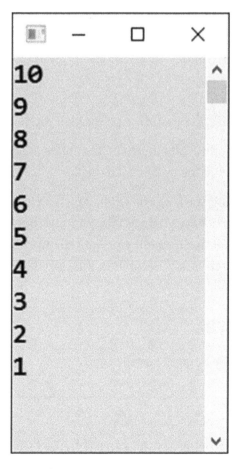

***Figure 22-2.*** *Numbers going down*

## Solution

Here's the code:

```
static void Main(string[] args)
{
    // Output
    for (int number = 10; number >= 1; number--)
    {
        Console.WriteLine(number);
    }

    // Waiting for Enter
    Console.ReadLine();
}
```

## Discussion

Note the following:

- The loop's *initializer* is possibly the simplest. You just start at ten.

- The *iterator* is not difficult either; the numbers go down, which is why you just subtract 1 at the end of each turn.

- The most difficult is the *loop condition*. You have to formulate it in such a way that it holds as long as you want the loop to go on and that it ceases holding at the moment you want to quit. The correct test is whether the number variable is greater than or equal to 1.

# Decimal Numbers

A series with decimal numbers might surprise you.

# Task

In this task, you will generate a series from 9 to 0 with the numbers decreasing by 0.9 in every step (see Figure 22-3).

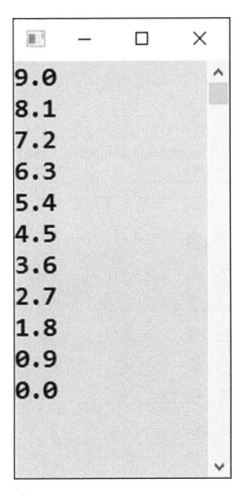

*Figure 22-3.* *Decreasing by 0.9*

## Seemingly Correct Solution

Using the style of the previous exercise, you could write the following:

```
static void Main(string[] args)
{
    // Output
    for (double number = 9; number >= 0; number -= 0.9)
    {
        Console.WriteLine(number.ToString("N1"));
    }
```

```
    // Waiting for Enter
    Console.ReadLine();
}
```

## Testing

However, testing discloses the missing last member of the series: 0 (see Figure 22-4).

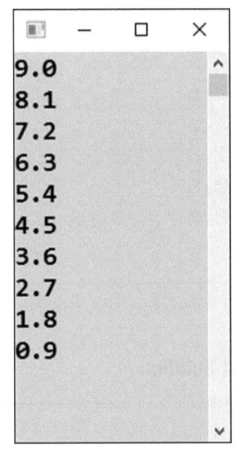

***Figure 22-4.*** *Missing last number*

How can that be?

# The Cause of the Error

The exercise shows how working with decimal numbers can be tricky; you need to be careful because decimal arithmetic can be imprecise!

You can sense the cause when you omit the formatting on a single decimal place (`.ToString("N1")`). Try it (see Figure 22-5).

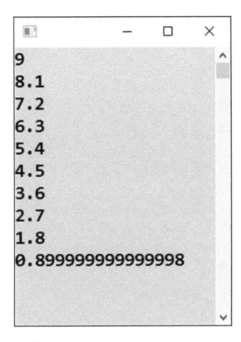

**Figure 22-5.** *Omitting the formatting*

You can see that the expected second-to-last series member is slightly less than it is supposed to be. Further subtraction of 0.9 gets you slightly below zero, which is why the expected last zero is not displayed.

# Correct Solution

Working with decimal numbers, you need to specify a loop's terminal value with a slight free play.

The correct solution of the exercise thus looks like this:

```
static void Main(string[] args)
{
    // Output
    for (double number = 9; number >= -0.0001; number -= 0.9)
    {
        Console.WriteLine(number.ToString("N1"));
    }

    // Waiting for Enter
    Console.ReadLine();
}
```

Check the result!

# Second Powers

Now, what about displaying two connected numbers in a single line?

## Task

In addition to numbers in a 1 to 10 series, you can display the corresponding second power in every line of output (see Figure 22-6).

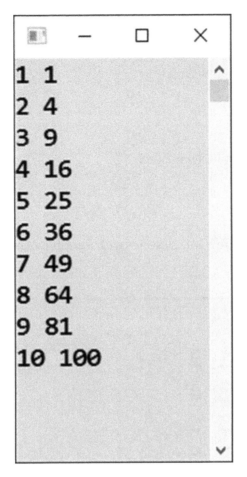

*Figure 22-6.* *Displaying the second power*

## Solution

Here's the code:

```
static void Main(string[] args)
{
    // Output
    for (int number = 1; number <= 10; number++)
    {
        int secondPower = number * number;
        Console.WriteLine(number.ToString() + " " + secondPower.
        ToString());
    }
```

```
    // Waiting for Enter
    Console.ReadLine();
}
```

# Two in a Row

Let's stay with two numbers in a line here.

## Task

In this task, you will generate a 1 to 20 series with a couple of numbers in every line of output (see Figure 22-7).

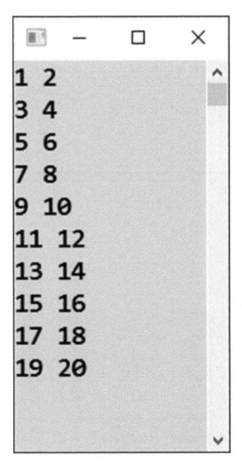

**Figure 22-7.**  *Displaying more than one number on a line*

# Solution

This exercise closely resembles the task of the alternating loop from the previous chapter. It can be solved in a number of ways, too. I will choose one of them: you will add a space after an odd number and a line break after an even number.

Here's the code:

```
static void Main(string[] args)
{
    // Output
    for (int number = 1; number <= 20; number++)
    {
        Console.Write(number);

        // What goes after the number depends on even/odd test
        if (number % 2 != 0)
        {
            // Odd number, displaying space
            Console.Write(" ");
        }
        else
        {
            // Even number, new line
            Console.WriteLine();
        }
    }

    // Waiting for Enter
    Console.ReadLine();
}
```

# Two Independent Series

Another interesting case that you might meet some day is the case of two independent series.

# Task

You will have two, a bit arbitrary, number series with a different count of members. The first one is descending by 2 in every step (111, 109, ..., 97), and the second one is ascending by 3 in every step (237, 240, ..., 270).

The program will display both a number from the first series and a number from the second series in every row (see Figure 22-8).

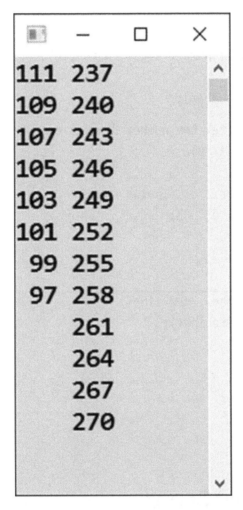

***Figure 22-8.*** *More complex alternating*

# Solution

Here's the code:

```
static void Main(string[] args)
{
    // Preparation
    int first = 111;

    // Output
    for (int second = 237; second <= 270; second += 3)
    {
        // Preparing first text
        string firstText = first >= 97 ?
            first.ToString().PadLeft(3) : "    ";

        // Actual output
        Console.WriteLine(firstText + " " + second.ToString());

        // Changing x
        first -= 2;
    }

    // Waiting for Enter
    Console.ReadLine();
}
```

# Discussion

Note the following:

- One of the series (the longer one) is displayed using the loop's control variable. The other one uses another independent variable.

- In every step, you check whether the shorter series still goes on.

- To achieve some nice formatting, you use the PadLeft method call, which adds spaces to the left of its parameter to reach the specified total number of characters.

# Summary

In this chapter, you practiced loops on tasks of generating various number series. Specifically, you learned the following:

- How to write the loop's iterator when the series is stepping by 2.

- How to display in a loop's body not directly the control variable but the value derived (calculated) from it.

- How to generate a descending series using the - - operator in a loop's iterator and specify the loop condition using the >= operator so that it is fulfilled as long as you want to do looping.

- That decimal number series require extra care because of the imprecise representation of decimal numbers in memory. This means, for example, that you need to provide an extra free play in the loop condition.

You also solved cases with two numbers in a single output row, with the more difficult final task of two independent series.

# CHAPTER 23

# Unknown Number of Repetitions

In all the loops you have solved so far, you knew the number of repetitions. Sometimes you did not know it when writing a program because the user was supposed to enter it. However, in all the cases, when a loop started, it had already been determined how many times it would repeat.

Sometimes the number of repetitions is not known at the moment a loop starts executing. Frequently you will be concerned with the question of whether a loop should go on or terminate.

## Entering a Password

The first task concerns logging in. You do not know in advance how many attempts the user will need.

## Task

You will repeatedly ask the user to enter a password until the user enters the correct one (see Figure 23-1). The correct password will be *friend*.

© Radek Vystavěl 2017
R. Vystavěl, *C# Programming for Absolute Beginners*, https://doi.org/10.1007/978-1-4842-3318-4_23

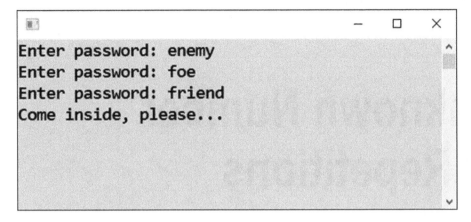

***Figure 23-1.*** *Repeatedly asking a question*

## Solution

Here's the code:

```
static void Main(string[] args)
{
    string correctPassword = "friend";

    bool ok; // the variable must be declared outside of the loop!
    do
    {
        // Input
        Console.Write("Enter password: ");
        string enteredPassword = Console.ReadLine();

        // Evaluating
        ok = enteredPassword == correctPassword;
    } while (!ok); // loop repeats when the condition holds

    Console.WriteLine("Come inside, please...");

    // Waiting for Enter
    Console.ReadLine();
}
```

# do-while Construction

To write the loop, you use the do-while construction.

The computer enters the loop after the word do, executes its statements, and asks "Once more?" If the condition after the while word holds, the computer returns to the beginning of the loop, in other words, after the do word. And so on.

The loop terminates at the moment when its condition after the while word is evaluated as unfulfilled (false).

# This Case

In this case, the program evaluates the entered password after each input. The evaluation result is then stored in a bool-typed variable called ok.

You want the loop to go on if the entered password is not correct. That is why you use a negation operator (an exclamation mark) in the while condition.

# Variable Outside of the Loop

C# requires that all variables used in the loop condition be declared outside of the loop. When you declare them inside, they are not visible when formulating the condition.

# Tip

Visual Studio can help you with your do-while loops. Just enter do and press the Tab key twice.

# Waiting for Descend

Imagine the computer watches some quantity that grows most of the time, and the task is to detect the (possibly rare) moment when it lessens (descends).

You would usually encounter such a problem when digging through a large amount of data stored in a file or in a database. However, you will solve this on some data entered by the user.

# Task

You will make a program that repeatedly asks the user for input (see Figure 23-2). Whenever the user enters a number less than the previous one, the program will notify the user (and terminate).

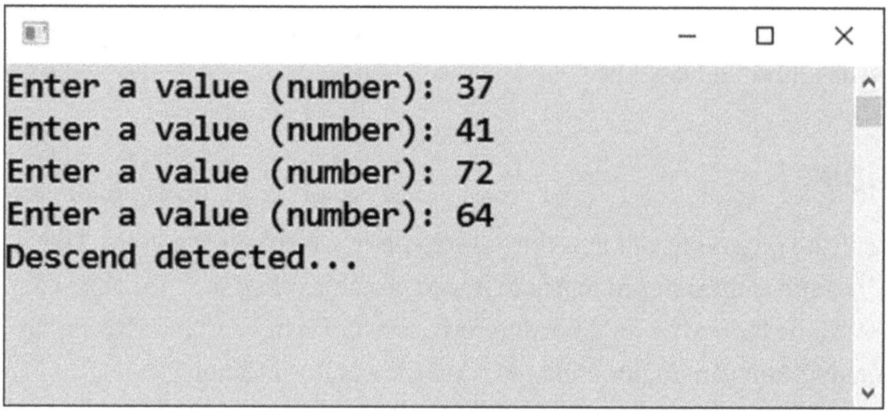

*Figure 23-2.* Terminating when the number gets smaller

# Solution

The core of the solution is to remember the previous value, not just the value currently entered.

Here's the code:

```
static void Main(string[] args)
{
    // Preparations
    int previous = int.MinValue;
    bool ok;

    // Repeating until descend
    do
    {
        // Input
        Console.Write("Enter a value (number): ");
        string input = Console.ReadLine();
        int value = Convert.ToInt32(input);
```

```
    // Evaluating
    ok = value >= previous; // ok = still not descending

    // Storing for the next round of the loop
    previous = value;
} while (ok);

    // Message to the user
    Console.WriteLine("Descend detected...");

    // Waiting for Enter
    Console.ReadLine();
}
```

## Discussion

The first value is somewhat special because it has no predecessor. Its absence can be circumvented by simulating it using some very small number. C# offers you `int.MinValue`, which is the least value that can be stored in the `int` type, which is minus two billion approximately.

## Every Week Until the End of Year

Let's proceed to the next exercise, which has to do with dates.

## Task

The task is to display dates until the year's end starting with today and proceeding in one-week steps (see Figure 23-3).

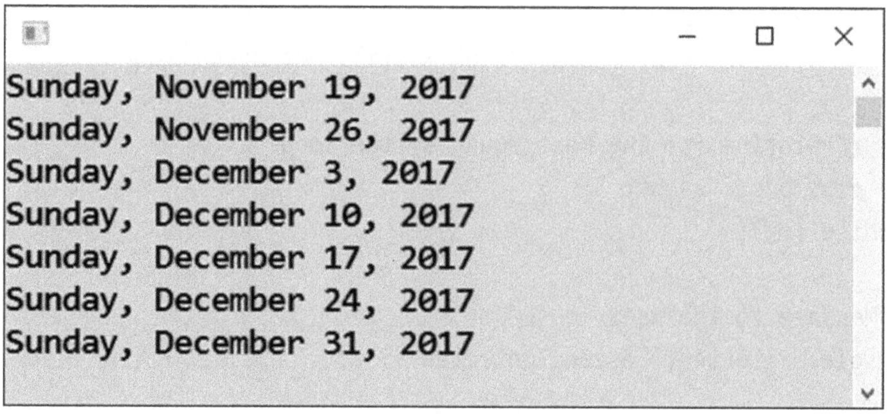

```
Sunday, November 19, 2017
Sunday, November 26, 2017
Sunday, December 3, 2017
Sunday, December 10, 2017
Sunday, December 17, 2017
Sunday, December 24, 2017
Sunday, December 31, 2017
```

*Figure 23-3.* *Stepping through the year, one week at a time*

## Solution

Here's the code:

```
static void Main(string[] args)
{
    // Today
    DateTime today = DateTime.Today;
    int thisYear = today.Year;

    // Repeating
    DateTime date = today;
    do
    {
        // Output
        Console.WriteLine(date.ToLongDateString());

        // Preparing next output (a week later)
        date = date.AddDays(7);
    } while (date.Year == thisYear);

    // Waiting for Enter
    Console.ReadLine();
}
```

# As Long As a 6 Is Being Thrown

Random numbers can provide you with other nice examples of the uncertain termination of a loop.

## Task

You will throw a die and keep throwing it as long as there is a 6 (see Figure 23-4 and Figure 23-5).

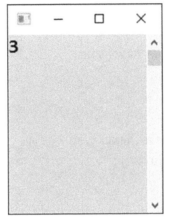

***Figure 23-4.*** *Rolling a die once (no 6, no repetitions)*

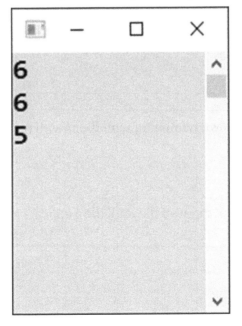

***Figure 23-5.*** *Rolling a die as long as you have a 6*

You may know some board game where this principle is used.

## Solution

Here's the code:

```csharp
static void Main(string[] args)
{
    // Random number generator
    Random randomNumbers = new Random();

    // Throwing as long as we have six
    int thrown;
    do
    {
        thrown = randomNumbers.Next(1, 6 + 1);
        Console.WriteLine(thrown);
    } while (thrown == 6);

    // Waiting for Enter
    Console.ReadLine();
}
```

# Until Second 6

This task is about the unknown number of repetitions with random values.

## Task

You will write a program that throws a die until the 6 appears for the second time (see Figure 23-6).

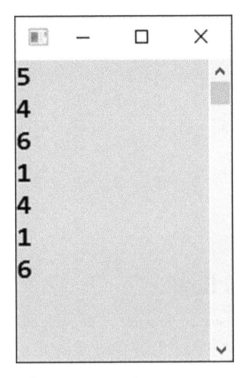

**Figure 23-6.** *Waiting until a 6 appears twice*

## Solution

You simply count the 6s.

Here's the code:

```
static void Main(string[] args)
{
    // Random number generator
    Random randomNumbers = new Random();

    // Throwing until the second six is thrown
    int howManySixes = 0;
    do
    {
        // Actual throwing
        int thrown = randomNumbers.Next(1, 6 + 1);
        Console.WriteLine(thrown);
```

```
    // Counting sixes
    if (thrown == 6)
    {
        howManySixes++;
    }
} while (howManySixes < 2);

    // Waiting for Enter
    Console.ReadLine();
}
```

# Until Two 6s in a Row

Do you know why there are so many examples of throwing dice? I liked to play board games when I was a kid, can you tell?

## Task

In this program, you will be throwing a die until a 6 is thrown twice in a row (see Figure 23-7).

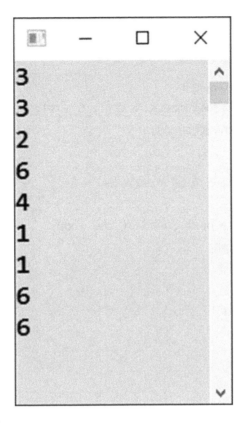

*Figure 23-7.* *Two 6s in a row*

## Solution

Besides the currently thrown number, you have to track the previous one as well. This is similar to the program in the "Waiting for Descend" section.

If both the current and previous numbers are 6s, the program terminates.

Again, the first value is specific in not having a predecessor. That is why the `previous` variable starts with 0, which is a value that can never appear on a die.

Here's the code:

```
static void Main(string[] args)
{
    // Random number generator
    Random randomNumbers = new Random();

    // Preparations
    int previous = 0;
    bool ending;
```

```
    // Throwing until two sixes in a row
    do
    {
        // Actually throwing
        int thrown = randomNumbers.Next(1, 6 + 1);
        Console.WriteLine(thrown);

        // Evaluating
        ending = thrown == 6 && previous == 6;

        // Preparing for next round of the loop
        previous = thrown;
    } while (!ending);

    // Waiting for Enter
    Console.ReadLine();
}
```

# Summary

In this chapter, you studied loops with the number of repetitions not known at the time the loops start. In C#, this kind of loop can be suitably written using the do-while construct. Its function is first to execute the statements of its body and then to ask "Once more?" You evaluate the condition, and if it holds, you execute another round of the loop.

You also saw that to use some variable in a do-while loop condition, the variable must be declared outside of the loop.

A frequent mistake when using the do-while loop is the wrong formulation of its condition. You have to be careful and write it in such a way that if you want to continue looping, the condition should evaluate to true.

In a couple of tasks of this chapter, you needed some value from the previous round of a loop. For this purpose, you used a special variable where you stored the value. Of course, the first round of the loop required special treatment.

# CHAPTER 24

# Accumulating Intermediate Results

In this chapter, you will study the important case of using loops to process large sets of data. You will often use a loop to go through a large amount of data to accumulate (aggregate) some intermediate result, which becomes the final result after the loop terminates.

## Sum of the Entered Numbers

A typical task in this category is summing a lot of values.

## Task

Say the user is entering numbers, with the last one being 0. In other words, users indicate they are finished by entering 0. The program then displays the sum of all the entered numbers (see Figure 24-1).

© Radek Vystavěl 2017
R. Vystavěl, *C# Programming for Absolute Beginners*, https://doi.org/10.1007/978-1-4842-3318-4_24

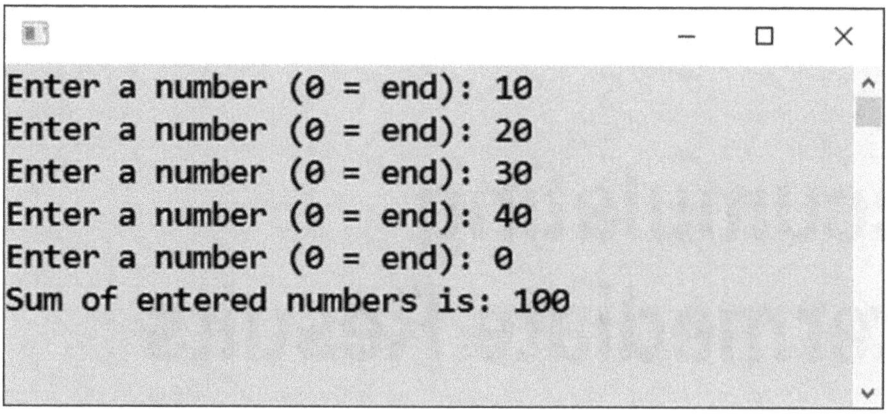

**Figure 24-1.** *Summing all numbers until 0*

## Solution

The solution's core is accumulating the intermediate result. You have to keep it in a variable and to add every entered number into that variable. As soon as the user terminates the input, the variable will contain the overall sum of all the entered values.

Here's the code:

```
static void Main(string[] args)
{
    // Preparations
    int sum = 0;
    int number;

    // Entering numbers until zero
    do
    {
        // Input
        Console.Write("Enter a number (0 = end): ");
        string input = Console.ReadLine();
        number = Convert.ToInt32(input);

        // Adding to intermediate sum
        sum += number;

    } while (number != 0);
```

```
    // Output
    Console.WriteLine("Sum of entered numbers is: " + sum.ToString());

    // Waiting for Enter
    Console.ReadLine();
}
```

# Product of the Entered Numbers

What about multiplying the entered numbers instead of summing them? Do you think the task is the same? It's not completely.

## Task

In this program the user enters numbers, with the last one being 0 (see Figure 24-2). The program then displays the product of all the entered numbers, with the exclusion of the final 0, obviously, which would make everything 0.

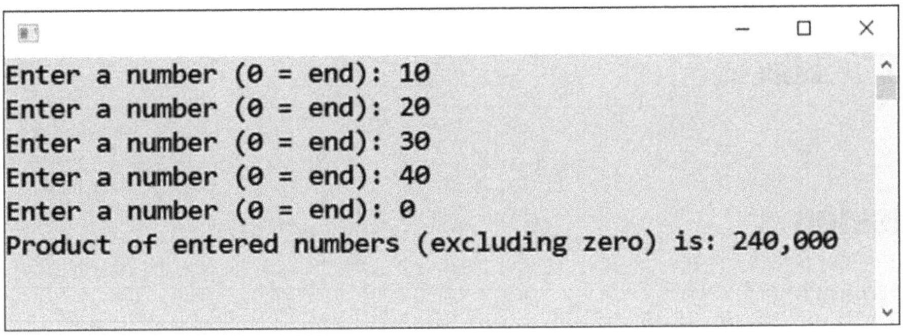

```
Enter a number (0 = end): 10
Enter a number (0 = end): 20
Enter a number (0 = end): 30
Enter a number (0 = end): 40
Enter a number (0 = end): 0
Product of entered numbers (excluding zero) is: 240,000
```

*Figure 24-2.* *Multiplying all numbers*

## Solution

Here's the code:

```
static void Main(string[] args)
{
    // Preparations
    double product = 1;
    int number;
```

```
// Entering numbers until zero
do
{
    // Input
    Console.Write("Enter a number (0 = end): ");
    string input = Console.ReadLine();
    number = Convert.ToInt32(input);

    // Accumulating in intermediate product (but not the last zero!)
    if (number != 0)
    {
        product *= number;
    }
} while (number != 0);

// Output
Console.WriteLine("Product of entered numbers (excluding zero) is: " +
product.ToString("N0"));

// Waiting for Enter
Console.ReadLine();
}
```

## Discussion

Note the following:

- The product variable starts at a value of 1 contrary to 0, which you used when calculating the sum.

- When updating the product, you need to take care not to include the final 0.

- You declare the product variable in type double for the result not to overflow. When you multiply, you quickly get big numbers.

# The Greatest

Another typical task when processing a large amount of data is searching for the extremes, in other words, the maximum or the minimum.

## Task

In this program, the user enters ten numbers. The program then outputs which one is the greatest (see Figure 24-3).

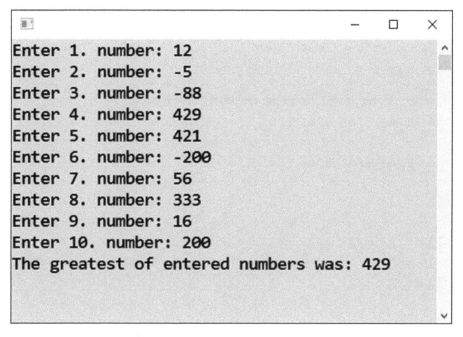

```
Enter 1. number: 12
Enter 2. number: -5
Enter 3. number: -88
Enter 4. number: 429
Enter 5. number: 421
Enter 6. number: -200
Enter 7. number: 56
Enter 8. number: 333
Enter 9. number: 16
Enter 10. number: 200
The greatest of entered numbers was: 429
```

***Figure 24-3.*** *Outputting the greatest number*

## Solution

You are going to accumulate the intermediate result again. This time it will be the greatest number "so far." You have to take special care with the first value; the greatest variable is set to the least possible value at the beginning in order to ascertain that the first entered number is always greater.

Because you expect exactly ten values in the input, it is more convenient to use the for loop here.

Here's the code:

```
static void Main(string[] args)
{
    // Preparation
    int greatest = int.MinValue;

    // Input of ten numbers
    for (int order = 1; order <= 10; order++)
    {
        // Input
        Console.Write("Enter " + order.ToString() + ". number: ");
        string input = Console.ReadLine();
        int number = Convert.ToInt32(input);

        // Is it greater than the greatest so far?
        if (number > greatest)
        {
            greatest = number;
        }
    }

    // Output
    Console.WriteLine("The greatest of entered numbers was: " + greatest.
    ToString());

    // Waiting for Enter
    Console.ReadLine();
}
```

# The Second Greatest

What about the second greatest value? This is a substantially more difficult exercise.

# Task

The task is to choose the second greatest number out of the ten entered ones (see Figure 24-4).

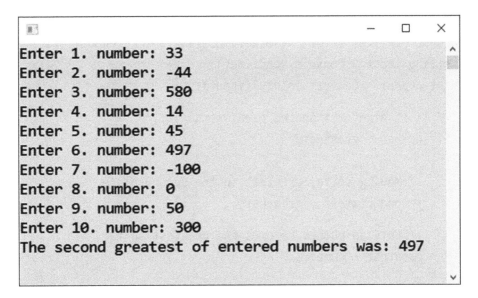

*Figure 24-4.* *Displaying the second greatest number*

## Solution

You need to remember and continuously update the two greatest numbers greatest. It would not be enough to remember just the second greatest.

The situation resembles a ski competition, with the competitors arriving to the finish line one after another. At a certain moment, someone is the first. Afterward, someone else pushes the first out to the second place. Possibly in a later time, that skier may lose even the second place because someone else will be better than him, or even better than the new leader.

Here's the code:

```
static void Main(string[] args)
{
    // Preparation
    int greatest = int.MinValue;
    int secondGreatest = int.MinValue;

    // Input of ten numbers
    for (int order = 1; order <= 10; order++)
    {
```

```
    // Input
    Console.Write("Enter " + order.ToString() + ". number: ");
    string input = Console.ReadLine();
    int number = Convert.ToInt32(input);

    // Is it greater than the greatest so far?
    if (number > greatest)
    {
        // Moving so far greatest to the second place
        secondGreatest = greatest;

        // Entered number becomes the greatest so far
        greatest = number;
    }
    else
    {
        // We did not beat the greatest, will we beat the second
            greatest at least?
        if (number > secondGreatest)
        {
            secondGreatest = number;
        }
    }
}

// Output
Console.WriteLine("The second greatest of entered numbers was: " +
secondGreatest.ToString());

// Waiting for Enter
Console.ReadLine();
}
```

# Output of All Entered Names

The final exercise of the chapter is concerned with text, specifically processing a large amount of text (see Figure 24-5).

```
Enter person: Amy
Enter person: Brandon
Enter person: Celia
Enter person: David
Enter person: Eve
Enter person: Francis
Enter person:
Entered persons: Amy, Brandon, Celia, David, Eve, Francis
In reversed order: Francis, Eve, David, Celia, Brandon, Amy
```

*Figure 24-5.* *Printing in the original order and then reversed*

## Task

You will write a program that repeatedly reads the names entered by the user. The empty input signals the termination. The program then repeats all the entered names, first in the same order and then in the reversed order.

## Solution

So that you are able to repeat all the names at the end, you need to remember them somewhere. You need to *accumulate* them. One variable will accumulate them at its end (the same order output) and the other one at its beginning (the reversed order output).

Here's the code:

```
static void Main(string[] args)
{
    // Preparation
    string inSameOrder = "";
    string inReversedOrder = "";
    bool terminating;
```

```
    // Repeating until blank input
    do
    {
        // Input
        Console.Write("Enter person: ");
        string person = Console.ReadLine();

        // Processing input
        terminating = person.Trim() == "";
        if (!terminating)
        {
            inSameOrder = inSameOrder + person + ", ";
            inReversedOrder = person + ", " + inReversedOrder;
        }

    } while (!terminating);

    // Removing trailing comma and space
    if (inSameOrder.EndsWith(", "))
    {
        int numberOfCharacters = inSameOrder.Length;
        inSameOrder = inSameOrder.Remove(numberOfCharacters - 2);
    }
    if (inReversedOrder.EndsWith(", "))
    {
        int numberOfCharacters = inReversedOrder.Length;
        inReversedOrder = inReversedOrder.Remove(numberOfCharacters - 2);
    }

    // Output
    Console.WriteLine("Entered persons: " + inSameOrder);
    Console.WriteLine("In reversed order: " + inReversedOrder);

    // Waiting for Enter
    Console.ReadLine();
}
```

# Discussion

Note the following:

- You use the `Trim` method to cut off possible leading and trailing spaces of the entered text in order to allow termination with any blank input, including several spaces.

- At the end, you have to get rid of the last two characters in both accumulated pieces of text. Before doing it, you test whether these two characters (a comma and a space) appear at the end of the text at all. These characters will not be there if the user immediately terminates the program by entering a blank line.

- To test whether text ends with something, you use the `EndsWith` method.

# Summary

One of the most frequent usages of loops is processing large amounts of data, be it numbers, text, or whole objects. In the loop's body, you process a single piece of data, while the loop ascertains that all the data gets its turn.

You practiced processing larger amounts of data with examples of summing, multiplying, and finding extremes.

The most difficult exercise was that of finding the second greatest number, which required careful thinking about the possible situation that may arise depending on the data.

The last task showed you several methods to cope with text: `Trim`, `EndsWith`, and `Remove`.

# CHAPTER 25

# Advanced Loops

In this chapter, you will complete the topic of simple loops. That's simple in a sense of "not nested," not in a sense of "trivial." No loops are trivial, especially the loops in this chapter.

The chapter and the whole book will close with a bonus: a moon landing simulation game. If you find the exercises in this chapter too difficult, play the game only.

## Thank God It's Friday (TGIF)

It is time to get acquainted with the while loop, which is a cousin of the do-while loop you are already familiar with.

## Task

You will prepare a program that displays the date of the nearest Friday and the number of days remaining (see Figure 25-1).

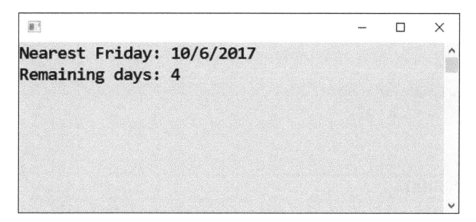

**Figure 25-1.** *Displaying the nearest Friday*

© Radek Vystavěl 2017

R. Vystavěl, *C# Programming for Absolute Beginners*, https://doi.org/10.1007/978-1-4842-3318-4_25

# Solution

Here's the code:

```
static void Main(string[] args)
{
    // Today's date
    DateTime today = DateTime.Today;

    // Moving day after day until hit on Friday
    DateTime date = today;
    while (date.DayOfWeek != DayOfWeek.Friday)
    {
        date = date.AddDays(1);
    }

    // Calculating remaining days
    TimeSpan dateDifference = date - today;
    int daysRemaining = dateDifference.Days;

    // Outputs
    Console.WriteLine("Nearest Friday: " + date.ToShortDateString());
    Console.WriteLine("Remaining days: " + daysRemaining.ToString());
    if (daysRemaining == 0)
    {
        Console.WriteLine("Thanks God!");
    }

    // Waiting for Enter
    Console.ReadLine();
}
```

# Discussion

Let's look at the program more closely.

## While Loop

To write the loop, you use the `while` construct, which is similar in function to `do-while`, except its condition is at the beginning. The condition is thus being evaluated for the first time *before* the loop is entered, and if it does not hold, the loop body is not executed even a single time!

## This Case

Testing the condition before entering the loop is exactly what you need to do. If today is Friday, you want to let it be untouched. Otherwise, you are adding one day.

## TimeSpan Object

When you subtract two dates, the result that arises is a `TimeSpan` object. Its `Days` property says how many days have passed during the "time span" between the two dates.

# Power

Loops are frequently practised in mathematical exercises.

## Task

You will write a program that calculates the *n*th power of the number *x* given the decimal *x* and the positive integer *n* on its input (see Figure 25-2).

```
Enter x (number to be raised): 2
Enter n (power): 10
x^n=1024
```

***Figure 25-2.*** *Calculating the nth power*

Just to remind you, $2^{10} = 2 \times 2 \times 2 \times 2 \times 2 \times 2 \times 2 \times 2 \times 2 \times 2 = 1024$, which is the number 2 repeated 10 times in the final product.

# Solution

The task can be solved using repeated multiplication by $x$. This means you use the intermediate result accumulation approach that you have already learned.

In principle, the solution is quite close to the one in the "Product of Entered Numbers" section.

```
static void Main(string[] args)
{
    // Inputs
    Console.Write("Enter x (number to be raised): ");
    string inputX = Console.ReadLine();
    double x = Convert.ToDouble(inputX);

    Console.Write("Enter n (power): ");
    string inputN = Console.ReadLine();
    int n = Convert.ToInt32(inputN);

    // Calculating
    double result = 1;
    for (int count = 0; count < n; count++)
    {
        result *= x;
    }

    // Output
    Console.WriteLine("x^n=" + result.ToString());

    // Waiting for Enter
    Console.ReadLine();
}
```

# Sine

Continuing with mathematics, do you know how a computer actually calculates, for example, the sine function? If you are into mathematics, you might be interested in it.

To perform the task, you can use a so-called Taylor expansion. Some smart people found that the value of the sine function at a given point $x$ ($x$ is an angle in radians) can be calculated as a sum of infinite series.

$$\sin x = x - \frac{x^3}{3!} + \frac{x^5}{5!} - \frac{x^7}{7!} + \cdots$$

# Task

The task now is to write a program that calculates the sum of this series and compares the result to the value of the ready-made method Math.Sin (see Figure 25-3).

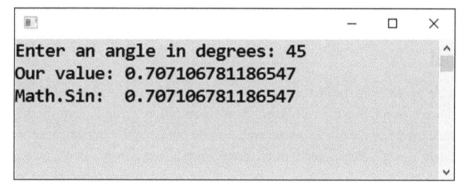

*Figure 25-3.* *Calculating sine*

If you are not interested in how to calculate the value of the sine function, use this task as a challenge to write a more difficult loop.

# Analysis

First, you have to analyze the calculation.

# Infinite Series

The series to be summed is infinite, but you may wonder how to sum an infinite number of numbers.

You cannot do this, of course. The trick is that you actually do not need to sum an infinite number of members of the series. At a certain point, they become so small that their contribution is somewhere far behind the decimal point.

For practical reasons, you need only a definite precision, say 15 decimal places; the `double` type does not accommodate more places anyway. You will thus be calculating the sum as long as the series members are greater than 1 on the 15th place after the decimal point.

# Series Members

All the series members are similar to one another. They have an odd power up, odd factorial down, and a changing sign.

To remind you, $7! = 1 \times 2 \times 3 \times \dots \times 7$. In other words, the factorial is the product of all the numbers from 1 to the number given.

# Factorial

It is possible to calculate the factorial in a way similar to how you calculated the power earlier in this chapter, in other words, progressively multiplying all the numbers in a loop.

However, you can do it in a smarter way. You do not need to calculate every factorial from scratch. You can always get it much faster from the previously calculated one.

For example, $7! = 7 \times 6 \times 5!$. The factorial of 7 can be calculated from the factorial of 5 by multiplying by "missing numbers" 6 and 7.

# Power

A similar trick can be used to calculate the "power part" of each series member. The power does not have to be calculated from scratch. The next power is simply the previous power times $x$ squared.

For example, $x^7 = x^5 \times x^2$.

# Solution

Here's the solution:

```
static void Main(string[] args)
{
    // Input
    Console.Write("Enter an angle in degrees: ");
    string input = Console.ReadLine();
    double angle = Convert.ToInt32(input);

    // Converting to radians
    double x = Math.PI / 180 * angle;

    // Preparations
    double member;
    double sum = 0;
    double tinyValue = 1e-15;

    double sign = 1;
    double power = x;
    double factorial = 1;
    double multiplier = 1;

    // Sum of the series
    do
    {
        // Calculating current member of the series
        member = sign * power / factorial;

        // Appending to sum
        sum += member;

        // Preparing next step
        sign *= -1;
```

```
        multiplier++;
        factorial *= multiplier;
        multiplier++;
        factorial *= multiplier;

        power *= x * x;

    } while (Math.Abs(member) > tinyValue);

    // Output
    Console.WriteLine("Our value: " + sum.ToString());
    Console.WriteLine("Math.Sin:  " + Math.Sin(x).ToString());

    // Waiting for Enter
    Console.ReadLine();
}
```

## Enhancement

You can make the calculation still better using the fact that the series converges the fastest for values of x around 0. The calculation for the big values of x could be converted to the small values of x using sine function symmetries.

I would think that Microsoft has this trick in the code of Math.Sin.

## Moon Landing

Ever since the Apollo 11 moon landing, creating a simulation of a lunar module landing has been popular on various programming platforms. So, you will write a similar simulation as the concluding task of this book.

# Task

You will write a program simulating the moon landing. It will keep track of the module's height $h$ above the moon's surface, the module's velocity $v$, and the mass $m_F$ of the fuel remaining for landing.

The user's task is to land softly (with the least possible velocity). In each step, representing one second of the landing maneuver, the user enters how much the braking should be applied based on a percentage. The higher the percent, the lower the velocity, but at the same time, the more fuel that's consumed, as shown in Figure 25-4.

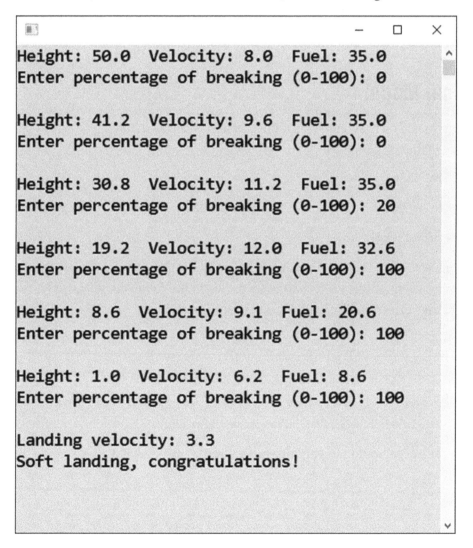

```
Height: 50.0  Velocity: 8.0  Fuel: 35.0
Enter percentage of breaking (0-100): 0

Height: 41.2  Velocity: 9.6  Fuel: 35.0
Enter percentage of breaking (0-100): 0

Height: 30.8  Velocity: 11.2  Fuel: 35.0
Enter percentage of breaking (0-100): 20

Height: 19.2  Velocity: 12.0  Fuel: 32.6
Enter percentage of breaking (0-100): 100

Height: 8.6  Velocity: 9.1  Fuel: 20.6
Enter percentage of breaking (0-100): 100

Height: 1.0  Velocity: 6.2  Fuel: 8.6
Enter percentage of breaking (0-100): 100

Landing velocity: 3.3
Soft landing, congratulations!
```

***Figure 25-4.*** *The moon landing program*

As soon as the height decreases below zero, the module has landed. The program notifies the user on the landing velocity and performs the evaluation according to the following table:

| Landing Velocity | Evaluation |
|---|---|
| Less than 4 m/s | Soft landing |
| 4–8 m/s | Hard landing |
| Greater than 8 m/s | † |

If all the fuel is consumed before the landing is over, the program starts ignoring the entered braking values, and the braking force is set to zero.

# Physical Model

The program will be based on the model of reality discussed here.

Here are the initial values:

- $h = 50$ (m)

- $v = 8$ (m/s)

- $m_F = 35$ (kg)

In each step representing one second of the landing maneuver, the values of the tracked physical quantities will change according to the following relations ($\Delta$ means the change of the corresponding quantity, as is usual in physics):

$\Delta h = -v - a/2$

$\Delta v = a$

$\Delta m_F = -F / 3000$

where

- The braking force is $F = 360 \times$ *percent of braking*.

- The acceleration toward the surface is $a = 1.62 - F / 8000$.

# Solution

Here's the code:

```
static void Main(string[] args)
{
    // Initial values
    double h = 50, v = 8, mF = 35;

    // Preparation
    bool malfunction = false;

    // Repeating individual landing steps
    while (h >= 0)
    {
        // Displaying current values
        string height   = "Height: " + h.ToString("N1");
        string velocity = "Velocity: " + v.ToString("N1");
        string fuel     = "Fuel: " + mF.ToString("N1");
        Console.WriteLine(height + "   " + velocity + "   " + fuel);

        // Input
        Console.Write("Enter percentage of breaking (0-100): ");
        string input = Console.ReadLine();
        double percents = 0;
        try
        {
            percents = Convert.ToDouble(input);
            if (percents < 0 || percents > 100)
            {
                malfunction = true;
            }
        }
```

```
        catch (Exception)
        {
            malfunction = true;
        }
        if (malfunction)
        {
            percents = 0;
            Console.WriteLine("CONTROL MALFUNCTION!");
        }

        // Fuel check
        if (mF <= 0)
        {
            percents = 0;
            Console.WriteLine("NO FUEL!");
        }

        // Calculating new values
        double F = 360 * percents;
        double a = 1.62 - F / 8000;
        h -= v + a / 2;
        v += a;
        mF -= F / 3000;
        if (mF <= 0)
        {
            mF = 0;
        }

        // Output of an empty line
        Console.WriteLine();

    } // End of a single landing step

    // Output
    Console.WriteLine("Landing velocity: " + v.ToString("N1"));
    string evaluation = v < 4 ?
        "Soft landing, congratulations!" :
        (v <= 8 ? "Hard landing." : "Houston, crew is lost...");
```

```
    Console.WriteLine(evaluation);

    // Waiting for Enter
    Console.ReadLine();
}
```

# Summary

This chapter closed the book with several examples of what might be considered advanced loops.

The first exercise was perhaps the easiest. It got you acquainted with the `while` loop, a close relative of the `do-while` loop you are already familiar with. The only difference is that the `while` loop has its condition at the beginning, which means it is being evaluated already before the loop is entered for the first time. Subsequently, the loop's body will never be executed in case the condition does not evaluate to `true` at the beginning.

This was precisely what you needed. If the present day was Friday, you did not want to execute the loop's body (moving a day further) even a single time; you wanted to stay with Friday.

The next task transferred you into the domain of mathematics. You exercised repeated multiplication and gradual result accumulation to get the $n$th power of a specified number.

The Sine task was probably the most difficult one of the whole book. I presented it here as a bonus for mathematically minded readers. You saw how the computer can calculate the values of what is called a *transcendent mathematical function*.

The sine values can be calculated using an infinite Taylor series. The trick is to truncate the series after the finite number of its members at the moment they are becoming too small to add anything to the final result considering the finite precision of decimal numbers in the computer.

The solution also showed you some tricks to get the calculation faster. You used previous series members to efficiently calculate the next ones.

The final moon landing task combined many things you learned throughout the book in a relaxing game you can enjoy!

# Personal Notes

Now that this book is at its end, allow me, please, a few personal notes. Programming is not only about computers, keywords, and algorithmic thinking. To me, it is a lifelong passion and personal.

## Dice

I noted already that there are lots of exercises in this book simulating dice throwing because I played lots of board games as a child. These were not just games purchased from a store. I invented many of my own games then, with most of them simulating sport events. There were different rules for sprints, long runs, jumps, bike races, soccer, and so on. That was possibly a good preparation for becoming a programmer.

## The Sine Task

I admit the Sine task of this chapter is substantially above a beginner's level. I included it to give you a glimpse at your possible future in the Wonderful Land of Programming.

To me, the task also has a personal connection. At some point when I was in school, I wondered how a calculator computes sines. I was thinking the function values are tabulated ("hardwired") in the calculator and further interpolated. Only later did I find out the other way, the one you saw.

## Moon Landing

A simplified version of the moon landing task was actually my first encounter with programming. No, I didn't program it; I was its computer instead.

When I was young, I read a special issue of a journal explaining programming to youngsters like me. The issue contained a paper computer. It was a piece of paper with windows representing variables. In these windows you could pull paper strips, writing a variable's values on them. Assigning a new value to a variable? You just pulled the strip to hide the old value and wrote down a new value on the same strip with a pencil.

I performed all the calculations using an electronic calculator. I was executing the program's statements, and I was the computer's CPU running at a marvelous speed of 0.5 Hz (yes, the G is omitted intentionally), which could be boosted to 0.6 Hz using a chocolate bar.

At that time, which was 1982 in Czechoslovakia, I landed that moon module possibly several hundred times, later also using my software on a programmable calculator. Perhaps I was the most experienced astronaut of the days. Regardless, that was a highly motivating road toward programming.

# Concluding Wish

To stay on a cosmic note, I hope I managed to launch you into your own programming orbit. Sometimes I went a bit deep, so maybe you will appreciate returning to the exercises and working through the book a few times. It's a way to refill the supplies of your cosmic station.

I wish you many joys and successes in your future programming!

# Index

© Radek Vystavěl 2017
R. Vystavěl, *C# Programming for Absolute Beginners*, https://doi.org/10.1007/978-1-4842-3318-4

# Get the eBook for only $5!

Why limit yourself?

With most of our titles available in both PDF and ePUB format, you can access your content wherever and however you wish—on your PC, phone, tablet, or reader.

Since you've purchased this print book, we are happy to offer you the eBook for just $5.

To learn more, go to http://www.apress.com/companion or contact support@apress.com.

# Apress®

DISCARD

CPSIA information can be obtained
at www.ICGtesting.com
Printed in the USA
LVHW01s1527190118
563149LV00009B/191/P